FREE
AGENT

FREE AGENT

INTANGIBLE ASSETS FOR OVERCOMING ADVERSITY AND TIMES OF TRANSITION

RENNIE CURRAN

FOREWORD BY MARK RICHT

Attention corporations, universities, colleges, and professional organizations:
Quantity discounts are available on bulk purchases of this book for educational, gift purposes, or as premiums for increasing magazine subscriptions or renewals. Special books or book excerpts can also be created to fit specific needs.
Rennie Curran is available to speak at your next event.

To Contact Author: Rennie Curran, Former Athlete/ Motivational Speaker/Coach/Entrepreneur

www.RennieCurran.com | Twitter -@Renniecurran53| Instagram- @RennieCurran | Youtube – LiberianDream35

Book Cover Design By Dalton Patterson © 2013 Fuze Media Design
WWW.RATHSIPUBLISHING.COM
INFO@RATHSIPUBLISHING.COM

Printed in the United States of America.

What others are saying about *Free Agent*

"As a former UGA player who also wore the number 35 I found it quite intriguing to follow his career both at UGA and in the pros. I have always admired his hard work and determination which propelled him both on the field and off. 'Success comes before work only in the dictionary' and Rennie Curran is a true living testimony .... Cheers"

Verron Haynes
Former UGA Fullback, ESPN International Commentator, Model

"I have long admired Rennie Curran as a football player at the University of Georgia. I further admire him for turning his disappointing NFL aspirations into an inspiring playbook for the many people who have and will face disappointments in the pursuit of their dreams. Rennie wants to inspire people to chase their 'dreams again'."

Vince Dooley
Former Legendary University of Georgia Coach, Public Speaker
Author, "Dooley: My 40 Years at Georgia."

"Over the past 30 years, I have had the privilege of working with over 1300 National Football League Players in speed and strength development. I have known Rennie since his middle school days, had the opportunity to train him while he was at Brookwood High School, and then while he was a star athlete at the University of Georgia.

I have gotten to know Rennie on a professional and personal level. I find him to be one of the most humble, loving, caring, individuals that I have ever met. He is a man of the highest character who truly puts the three F's in order: Faith, Family and Friends.

On a professional level, I have found that Rennie takes this Bible verse to heart, Colossians 3:23 "Whatever you do, work at it with all your heart, as working for the Lord, not for man." Rennie is one of the most focused, dedicated and hardest working athletes I have ever trained. He is a natural leader who leads by example and exemplifies integrity at the highest level.

Rennie is all about building relationships and is so very passionate about helping others. His mantra is Luke 12:48, "To whom much is given, much is required." When you have been blessed with fame and fortune, Rennie believes you need to return those blessings to those in need.

As I've watched Rennie develop into the man he is today, I've seen trials and tribulations come his way; being released from the Bucs, his struggle to get re-signed into the NFL, the struggles of being a single dad, and through it all, Rennie has maintained a positive attitude and has trusted in his faith that he is exactly where he is supposed to be.

As you read his story, know that all the daily struggles you face do not go away because you are a professional athlete and in some cases, those problems are compounded. Rennie is an outstanding father, son, brother, and to me, a very special friend, who I love like a son.

I trust that any athlete that reads this book will be challenged to work hard to obtain the highest level of success in life, not only on the football field, but also in the classroom. It's about building personal relationships and doing it with class and dignity, as Rennie has.

As you chase your dreams and aspirations, remember it's not the destination but the journey!"

Walk On!

Chip Smith
Owner Competitive Edge Sports
Author, "Football Training Like the Pros"
Trainer of Champions

"Rennie Curran is an infectious person. His will to work and succeed is contagious. I have had the pleasure to observe his leadership actions on the field and off the field since Rennie was in 10th grade. He is truly a special person and I have not met another like him."

Ryan Goldin
Owner G.A.T.A Training

"Rennie Curran's use of the free agent metaphor is insightful and innovative. His experiences provide him with a unique advantage in providing valuable and practical wisdom for youth and those seeking to succeed against the odds. A must read!"

Dr. Billy Hawkins, author of The New Plantation: Black Athletes, College Sports, and Predominantly White NCAA Institutions

"I had the chance to follow Rennie's football career over the course of his youth GFL playing days, through high school, University of Georgia and up to this point professionally. I always admired how Rennie took time out for younger athletes and students on and off the field. Curran is the kind of person you as a father would endorse your daughter to marry; which in my opinion is the highest endorsement a father could give. I truly believe the qualities and traits Rennie perfected during his adolescent years have and will pay dividends in real life when his professional playing days end."

Erik Richards, National Recruiting Director, US Army All-American Bowl, Gwinnett Football League President

"I was working a high school football camp when I first had the pleasure of meeting Rennie. Being a former NFL linebacker, I was immediately impressed by his muscular physique, his footwork, and his knowledge of the game. I followed his outstanding career at UGA, but I was even more impressed as I got to know him away from the gridiron. Rennie, I'm proud to call you a friend. Continue the good work on and off the field."

Jessie Tuggle
Former All-Pro Atlanta Falcons Linebacker

"Truly inspired! "Free agent" is not about sports, it's about life. We are all free agents at some point in our journey. Rennie lends readers a great mind state and life formula on how to deal with that situation when it is presented."

Marlon Wayans
Actor, Director, Writer, Comedian

"As a seasoned actor with over 20 years experience in the entertainment industry, I can honestly say "Free Agent" provides a breath of fresh air read that can be translated across different industries and sectors. Rennie Curran, I commend you for a great job with your first book and opening your personal life experiences to the world to serve as an influence!"

Carl Anthony Payne
Actor / Producer / Director

"A 10 year old boy walked down a hill one day to attend his first little league football practice. Little did we know that with God's blessing and a burning desire to succeed, Rennie would use his football career to affect so many people in a positive way. Even

now in the midst of his first real disappointment in the game he loves, he continues to strive to make those around him better."
"A quitter never wins, and a winner never quits."

The Benton's
Little League Coach and Family

"Rennie Curran's book is a must read! It helps to build character and determination in young people. It also serves as a stabilizing force in the lives of athletes. As one of his mentors, I see Rennie as a young person ahead of his time. His endurance, commitment and loyalty have aided him in going the limits. He is a shining example. As his big "bro", he is certainly the little brother that I am truly proud of. Kudos!!!!!!!"

Hannibal Navies
CEO/Founder 360 Football Academy

"Having had a similar NFL experience as Rennie, I can absolutely relate to the adversity and uncertainty Rennie writes about.....I think everyone at some point in their lifetime can relate to this, and I appreciate Rennie's willingness to share his experience in hopes it will inspire someone to get back up no matter how many times you get knocked down."

David Greene, (Former UGA Quarterback 01-04)

There are many reasons to admire Rennie Curran. He's an accomplished athlete with the trophies and accolades to prove it, but it's the courage he demonstrates off the field that impresses me most. Sharing his story will undoubtedly help countless children who need a light to show them the way. Curran can be that beacon of hope.

William James Brown
Son of "James Brown"

CONTENTS

FREE
AGENT

FOREWORD

I can remember waiting for the phone to ring. The NFL Draft was winding down and although many names had been called, my name and my phone wasn't called. At that moment I became an undrafted free agent. I figured my NFL journey had ended, before it had even begun. Thankfully I got a call from the Denver Broncos. After a short stint with the Denver Broncos and the Miami Dolphins my journey really began.

My former University of Georgia player, Rennie Curran, wrote this book using his personal experiences with life and athletics to help inspire others. In my opinion, it certainly is inspiring! I can relate to a lot of the experiences Rennie shares within this book. I truly believe everyone wants to achieve their dreams and after reading "Free Agent", readers will find the help they need.

Coach Mark Richt
University of Georgia Bulldogs

Introduction and Overview

I am writing this book at a time in my life where I am trying to realize what exactly my God-Given purpose is. I think I can identify with a lot of young adults in the fact that I'm fresh out of school ,trying to establish myself with a foundation that will last my entire life, but I don't even know where to start or where the choices I make in these next couple years will lead me. Writing this book has given me a totally separate channel to vent all of my emotions. If anyone had told me I would be writing my first book at the age of twenty-four, I would have straight up laughed in their face.

As a child I hated writing. Writing a two page paper always seemed worse than a trip to the dentist to get my teeth pulled. My teachers would have to force it out of me, and the worst part was my handwriting. It was not until I began writing about things I was passionate about that I truly began to appreciate the value and enjoyment you can have when writing. My first experiences of truly enjoying writing were telling stories of the memories of playing little league football. Also, I found relief in writing as a way of venting about losing a loved one. Of course I found other ways of making writing useful, especially when it came to the classic love letters. When it came to writing to a girl I liked, my writing abilities instantly became flawless.

I've spent the last thirteen years of my life doing the very thing I love - playing the game of football. It started off as pure love for the game at a young age, but through the years, many things have changed. It quickly changed from a game I played just for fun, into a job in order to provide for my family. The game of football has taught me a lot of life lessons in a way that the normal person never gets the chance to experience. Although I love the game of football, I realize it is merely something I was blessed to do, not who I am. Also, I realize the inevitability that football will one day come to an end. Hopefully it will be a smooth transition and not the suddenly tragic end experienced by many of my colleagues who have graced the field before me. That leaves me yearning with the question of what is my true purpose in life, and how football of all things fits into it. I always wonder why this dream was planted in me of all things.

My greatest hope for anyone reading this book is for them to put themselves in my shoes, replacing my dream with whatever dream they may have, and realize it is very much attainable if you can master the topics talked about in each chapter. Truly mastering these topics definitely won't change things overnight; it's a lifelong journey. I believe my book has a powerful message that can touch and inspire many different types of people. This book is intended for that high school kid in his junior year who is struggling with trying to find the right college to go to. Does he choose what his passion is or does he do what will please his parents and people around him? This book is for that college student who will soon be graduating and has no idea what they want to do in the real world. They have spent the past four years plus in college and feel like the only thing they have accumulated are Sallie Mae student loans. This book is intended for that hardworking adult who is married with a family to provide for and working a job that they absolutely cannot stand. They feel stuck in their situation and have simply forgotten what makes them happy because they have spent most of their lives trying to please others and being correct according to their given environment. If you have never been in any of these situations then I would like to congratulate you and ask you for some advice. If you are like the scenarios I just described, I would like you to be inspired, and to hopefully begin chasing your dreams again.

Dedication

I would like to first thank God for not only the opportunity to write this book, but also for the experiences that contributed to the contents of this book. I would not have had the courage to write this book if it weren't for his word, which clearly states that we are not given a spirit of fear and that I could do anything through him. I would like to thank my family for instilling in me the values, work ethic, and examples over the years, most of which I did not appreciate at the time of conception. Also, I would like to thank all of the teachers that forced me to write when I totally hated to. I now realize the importance of sharing my story and the positive impact that it can have on others. I would also like to thank all the people that ever criticized and doubted me. These certain individuals urged me to keep a chip on my shoulder and never get complacent.

I have been blessed to have so many people at different times in my life who took special interest in me before I was anything except a young child with a dream. My first and only little league coach, Ronnie Benton, brought out the best in me not only as a player, but as a person. His family became my second family. All of my numerous Brookwood high school and University of Georgia coaches; Chip Smith, owner of Competitive Edge Sports; Ryan Golden of GATA; Dr. Michael Hatrak of Synergy Release Sports; My pastor Rev. William B. G. K. Harris, who helped me by providing me with spiritual knowledge, I thank you all. I would need an entire chapter to truly dedicate and honor the angels that God placed in my life to help me through educating, reforming, and providing for me in times of need. To my daughter Eleana, whose birth reinforced my focus leaving me with only one option, to be successful, I especially thank you.

Chapter 1 - The Free Agent

In the world of professional football, a free agent is seen as someone who has the freedom to sign with any franchise; someone who isn't under contract to any specific team. As a free agent, you are ultimately in control of your own destiny. This can be a great opportunity if you are a veteran player who has established yourself with a reputation for being a leader and playmaker. At the same time, it can be a disadvantage for an undrafted rookie who has to go above and beyond just to be given the opportunity to practice with a new team.

Choosing exactly where to take that next step in your career is a major decision. There are so many questions you must answer in that time. Should I go to the place that pays me the most money? Should I stay close to my family? Should I play in a system that fits me the best? Pick the right place with the right system, and your career is sure to take off. Pick the wrong place, and it can possibly mean the beginning of your downfall.

One of the toughest transitions from college to the NFL is coming to the mental realization that the game you love is no longer something you're doing for fun; it is now your job. Because of this, it is important to be strategic in every decision you make. Almost overnight, you basically become the CEO of your own company (yourself), and you are responsible for the success or failure of that company.

After being released from the Tennessee Titans, I stepped into the world of free agency. Although I'd worked as hard as I could, my best just seemed to not be good enough. I knew I could excel against any opponent if given the right opportunity, but it did nothing to kill the feeling of disappointment.

It was the morning after our last preseason game when I received the call.

"Hello?" I answered.

"Coach wants to see you," said the voice on the other end of the line, "and bring your playbook."

I had heard many guys before me talk about the experience of being cut, but I never thought that day would ever come for me. I tried to talk myself into believing they wanted to tell me how good of a job I had done in the previous game, but the reality of my fate soon set in.

I immediately called my mother. She was excited as she picked up the phone, having no idea of the news she was about to receive.

"They cut me," I said.

"They what?" she asked with surprise in her voice.

"I'm coming home," I replied. "I'm not on the team anymore." Simply saying those words sent a streak of pain shooting down my chest.

After a short conversation with my mother, I began to get my mind prepared for my final trip to the Titans facility. I stood in the bathroom looking at my reflection in the mirror, trying to gather my composure before heading off to turn in my playbook. As I arrived at the facility, I found a line of guys who had unfortunately suffered the same fate as me. In the game of professional football, the day after that last preseason game is pretty much like Judgment Day. You see players with more than enough talent and ability getting sent home for one reason or another.

I walked into the head coach's office, shook his hand, and handed in my playbook. He spoke, but I couldn't process anything coming from his mouth. All I could think about was how hard I had worked. All I could feel was the mixture of anger, disappointment, and relief.

Once I left the coach's office, I said my goodbyes to everyone and arrived back at my locker. I found a large black trash bag resting on top of it. As I started cleaning out my locker, I began to think of all the hopes, the dreams, and the possibilities of what could have been. Although I was disappointed, I felt a surprising and unexplainable feeling of peace. I knew I had done everything in my power to succeed and realized that I couldn't do anything more than my best.

I returned home to Georgia to be with my family and most of all, my little girl. If there was one good thing that came as a result of becoming a free agent, it was the fact that I was finally able to be a full-time father. Before my release, the only time I would get to see my daughter was after home games on Sundays. Otherwise, I had to rely on Skype or the telephone to hear her voice for a couple minutes.

All the disappointment of the day disappeared when I saw her beautiful, smiling face running toward me as I walked into the house. I picked her up and immediately hugged her as tightly as I possibly could. She wrapped her arms around my neck and buried her face into my chest. She didn't say anything, but I knew exactly how she felt by the way she held me. "Daddy is home," I said, holding her in my arms.

It was nice to be home and see my family, but at the same

time my mind wandered. As I lay in my bed, in the same room where I had grown up, millions of thoughts passed through my mind. Was the path I had chosen the right one? What was I going to do now? Should I go back to school or should I continue pursuing my dreams? What will I do if football doesn't work out? The uncertainty of my situation forced me to analyze my entire life plan.

My time of uncertainty is similar to that experienced by so many people. Whether you are a young person getting ready to graduate from high school who is debating over what college to attend, that college student who just earned a degree and is ready to take the plunge into the real world, or an adult who has just been laid off from a job you have worked for years, we all share the same journey of trying to find ourselves in the face of uncertainty. No matter what career path we choose, we all eventually find ourselves at a crossroad point where we have to make decisions that will ultimately affect our entire lives. Although most of us will never play professional football, I believe we all play the role similar to a free agent at some point in our lives.

From the time we are born into this world until the time we die, most of us spend our entire lives searching for where we fit in. While searching, similar questions are bound to arise. What is our purpose? Why were we put here on earth and what are we meant to accomplish? These are the questions in life that lead me to believe that at the end of the day, we all, to some extent, can be considered free agents.

In my given situation, I had to lean on the tools obtained

from real life experiences in order to find myself and get through this crossroad point. Although I was afforded many great teachings through my family, my culture and my church, some of the most important life lessons came from my experiences on the football field. There are certain universal life principals talked about in this book that you must understand in order to grow into that person you want to become. Understanding these principals is part of what helped me in my time as a free agent.

I love being able to use the game of football to discuss, describe, and analyze different topics in life. When most people watch the game, they just see it as a bunch of gigantic athletes knocking each other around. Most mothers, like mine, are scared for their children to play the game of football because of the threat of injury. I don't even want to get started on the public perception of being a professional athlete, at least not yet. All of the stereotypes, perceptions, and assumptions about the game can overshadow the valuable life lessons the game provides. It is a shame that many of my colleagues fail to recognize the importance of our experiences on the gridiron and how the very things that make us successful on the field can apply to the real world when our playing days are finished.

Football, much like life, is a game of detail. Those of you who are football fans know that the difference between a win and a loss in a major game between two great teams can come down to just a few minor errors. The same can be said about life in general. One small change or wrong decision can completely alter our entire lives for better or worse. If you really understand the concept of the game of football and the training involved, you will quickly realize that a lot of the intangible assets it takes to be a successful athlete are the same necessary attributes required to be successful in any profession.

One of the many obvious assets the game of football teaches is the ability to work as a team. A variety of individuals who possess different beliefs, talents, and goals must come together in order to accomplish something great. Each person must give up their individuality and leave their ego at the door. There is no better feeling than knowing you can trust the guy next to you because he is working just as hard as you. At the same time, there is nothing worse than trying to work with someone who is selfish. No matter how talented they are individually, they almost always become a cancer to the team; destroying the chemistry needed to succeed. Are you someone who can be trusted or are you the person who is a cancer to your "team"?

I haven't been around that long, but when speaking with anyone who has ever played on a championship team, one theme always seems to remain the same; they will make some type of reference to how close the relationships were within the team. This leads me to believe that teamwork is crucial. If you look at any established institution and the individuals that make up that institution, the same concept stands true. Teamwork is at the forefront of success. Everyone has a role and they must hold themselves accountable to make sure they do the job they are paid to do. Sure, one individual job may seem more important than another depending on the mental and physical demands, and some may make more money than others. However, at the end of the day, each individual must come together in order to ensure the success and continued existence of their given institution. This is just one of the many assets I have learned to master by playing the game of football.

I love to compare football to the game of chess. The way a chess player analyzes and anticipates an opponent's next move is the same war that takes place between offensive and defensive coordinators during a game of pigskin. Each coordinator is given eleven pieces (players) that they must strategically place in the best position to be successful on every play. Whether a player is on the offensive or defensive side of the ball, there are certain clues that allow them to anticipate their opponent's intentions. Through hours upon hours of film study, they start to pick up on various tendencies and habits. Sometimes the slightest movements or stances can be indicators. These clues are very easily missed by the untrained eye. The ability to study the person in front of them, understand their strengths, and weaknesses can take a player from good to great. Some of the most spectacular plays that occur on the field are nothing more than the result of hours of film study and vigilant preparation colliding with the right opportunity at the right time. That same preparation and anticipation is also beneficial in other walks of life. Talk to anyone in the police or military and I guarantee they will explain the importance of understanding tendencies, habits and body language. A lot of times, it can mean the difference between life and death.

One of the goals I have for myself is to help those of you reading this book realize that almost everything in life translates when it comes to intangible tools, no matter what career or relationship you choose to pursue. The importance of the keyword intangible cannot be overstated. Character traits like self-confidence, humility, and discipline are some of the assets described in this book. These assets, if improved upon, will give you a great opportunity to be successful at anything you are truly passionate about. Throughout your life, you may encounter times of uncertainty, but having an understanding of these intangible assets will help you take the necessary steps forward. I could pull up a bunch of scientific research and statistics to show you the correlations, but since I am inviting you into my mind, I must present my own theories; theories which have resulted from a mixture of knowledge and life experience. We will soon delve deeper into these theories, but before we begin discussing any of the intangible assets, we must first start with the asset that connects us all.

Chapter 2 - Imagination and Dreaming

I could think of no better way to begin the rest of this book than by discussing two basic but essential elements of the human experience: imagination and dreaming.

Imagination is defined as the ability to form mental images, sensations, and concepts in a moment when they are not perceived through sight, hearing, or other senses. Dreaming is the term used to describe the experience of envisioned images, sounds or other sensations during sleep. The ability to imagine and dream is at the cornerstone of thinking about any future goal or endeavor. When faced with uncertainty, it helps when you can mentally circle back to the things you've always loved to do.

This may be hard for some, but I'd like for you to reflect on your childhood. Close your eyes and try to envision what life was like when you were young and the world was at your grasp; before you knew the rigor of bills, failed relationships and taxes. Remember when the simplest thing like a piece of candy made you happy? A lot of us don't because we are so wrapped up in our jobs, hardships, and other meaningless things in our lives. Now think about what you wanted to be when you grew up. Was it a doctor, lawyer or astronaut? Then ask yourself what happened to that dream or goal. Did you just simply grow out of it, did you become fearful of the amount of work it would take, or did you make yourself believe that your dream was simply impossible? These are some of the things that have always puzzled me when I think about life and where I'm at now. I find myself looking at everyday working people, the ones who look miserable, and I wonder why they look that way. What action, lack of action, or event took place that got them to that point? At what time do most people stop dreaming and settle for mediocrity in life? Becoming a free agent forced me to think about these questions and recall why I had chosen this path in the first place. I came to realize that no matter what career you choose to pursue in life, everything starts with a dream that is born from your imagination.

One summer weekend, I decided to clean out the storage room in my parents' house. There were boxes upon boxes cluttering up the room, full of shoes, clothes, and documents I hadn't seen in years. I began going through the boxes, discarding anything I considered useless. Suddenly, I ran across a box containing some documents that were from elementary school. I looked through the box and found a composition notebook full of memoirs I had written in the 5th grade. I spent the next two hours reading and reminiscing over the stories I had written and I couldn't help but to reflect on my childhood memories. Back then, nothing seemed impossible or out of reach as long as I could imagine it.

The first memoir I came across was about one of my greatest memories, playing little league football. I felt goose bumps slowly start to rise on my neck as I read about the games and winning the championship as a ten year old. In the next memoir, I had written about how I wanted to become a football star. A large grin spread across my face as I read and I started laughing to myself. A rush of memories flowed through my head as I thought of the days since my childhood. My grin and laughter quickly turned into a feeling of thankfulness as I realized how rare it was for me to have actually been able to live out my childhood dreams. I thought of how many guys I grew up and played ball with, many of whom had the same dreams as me, but were never able to turn those dreams into a reality.

Finding those boxes forced me to not only think about the good times I experienced, but of the hard times as well; hard times that I will explain in more detail later in the book. It also helped me remember what made me happy at a young age. I guarantee that if we all had a story describing what we were thinking and doing at a young age, we would remember what truly makes us happy in the purest form. For that moment, we would forget about our current troubles and remember the dreams that had once seemed so realistic.

I attended my first college football game at the tender age of ten years old and I remember the experience as if it happened yesterday. It was a Saturday afternoon in Athens, Georgia, and my little league coach, Ronnie Benton, brought me along with his son, J.T., who was my teammate and best friend. The streets were full with people of all colors, ages and sizes dressed in red and black. I walked through the streets aimlessly following the lead of my coach, his son, and the thousands of people around me. As the buildings cleared, we approached Sanford Stadium. I remember walking into that stadium and being overwhelmed as I saw the immense crowd of people filling the stands. I stood at the edge of the walkway leading to the seats, frozen with amazement and losing myself in the stadium lights. My eyes locked onto the field as I watched star players like Quincy Carter, Musa Smith, and Thomas Davis. At that very moment, a dream was planted in the mind of a ten year old. As I took in my surroundings, I told myself that I would one day wear the Georgia uniform and play on that field. I engrained that dream into my mind so hard I believed it was only a matter of time. I had convinced myself, consciously and subconsciously, that I would be a Georgia Bulldog. Failure was not an option as my dream instantly became an obsession. My coach and his son taught me all of the traditions, chants and superstitions of Georgia football. They had no idea that simply taking me to my first college football game would consequently plant a seed of inspiration inside of me that would grow into a lifelong dream.

When I think of imagination and dreaming, I think of my parents who immigrated to the United States with hopes of bettering not only themselves but their families. Much like many of the other immigrants who have traveled to the U.S. over hundreds of years, they left behind everything that was dear and familiar to them. They entered the country with nothing; relying only on faith, hope, and an amazing work ethic to chase their dreams. I am a proud product of the dreams they had when leaving their country of Liberia. I'm grateful that they were able to endure and sacrifice so that I could be given the opportunities I have today.

I've heard millions of stories about immigrants who leave their respective countries with amazing professional skills and abilities. Many times they lose track, forget about their goals, God-given gifts, and the dreams they once had as they struggle to adjust to a society that is unfamiliar to them. Over the years, I've become way too familiar with the story of the immigrant who left their country at a high ranking position, only to settle for working a subpar job far from the ones they had dreamt of when coming to this country.

The older I get, the more I realize the importance of imagination and dreaming in our society. I find myself staring at beautifully constructed buildings and realizing that someone had to first imagine them in their mind before they could ever materialize into a reality. I look at the variety of successful businesses and products in this world wondering what sparks someone's imagination to create. If they can imagine and create these wonderful things, why can't you or I do the same?

The only thing that can hold you back from imagining and creating anything is your own mental limitations. Some people have brilliant dreams and objects in their imagination; however, many people allow their own pessimism to shoot down those dreams before they can even become a completely processed thought. Others let the people in their lives limit their imaginations and dictate whether or not they can achieve their dreams. What needs to be realized is that you are the only person who can decide what can or cannot be accomplished.

When I am playing in games, there are certain times when I simply visualize and imagine what I am going to do before the play even begins. Through preparation, ability, and confidence I am able to see myself making the play before the ball is snapped. I can say with full honesty that this type of imagination and subconscious prediction has helped me with my successes on the field. I believe the same principle can be applied to someone battling numerous circumstances in life. If you can allow your conscious mind to imagine yourself as a success in your chosen field while backing that up with preparation and confidence, it will only have a positive effect on your given situation.

Imagination and dreaming are the keys unlocking the doors that turn the impossible into the possible. When looking at your uncertain situation as a free agent, never underestimate your imagination, your dreams, and what makes you happy.

Chapter 3 - Self-Motivation - Pushing your Dreams

I believe there can be no achievement or retention of any of your dreams without understanding the topic of self-motivation. As a free agent, self-motivation is an essential asset. Self-motivation is defined by the initiative to undertake or continue a task or activity without another's prodding or supervision. This is huge when striving to achieve your dreams and finding yourself in life. One of the many reasons why people never really seem to get what they want out of life is because they lack the ability to self-motivate. No one can overcome the numerous challenges in life without possessing a burning desire to achieve. This desire must come from within; not from any outside sources such as friends, parents, or coaches. If another person wants to help you achieve a life goal that you don't really care about on a personal level, then all of their efforts will likely have little to no impact on you at the end of the day. You can listen to the world's best motivational speakers and literally be given all the tools needed to succeed, but unless you possess the self-motivation to take action, then no amount of advice will be useful advice.

When I think back on my childhood, I can clearly remember all the things I was personally motivated to accomplish. There were certain activities nobody had to force me to do simply because I was excited and enthusiastic about them. When it came to playing video games, enjoying recess, or watching Power Rangers I devoted an endless amount of energy that never seemed to diminish. No one had to tell me to do those things and no one could control or tame my addiction to those activities. However, when it came to studying, church, or doing chores I could never seem to find enough energy or focus. I always needed some form of motivation to do those things. Taking away my privileges or a spanking from my parents quickly gave me the motivation required to do what I needed to do. I laugh about it now as I got some serious spankings back in the day that I definitely deserved!

Growing up, I enjoyed many different activities, but nothing compared to football. I can still recall the morning when I convinced my parents to let me play a sport they saw as nothing more than a bunch of men destroying and mauling each other. I was nine years old at the time; stubborn and full of energy. I completely remember harassing my parents until they had no choice but to give in to my demands. That morning, my dad was in the middle of showering when I burst into my parents' room unannounced and proceeded to bang on the bathroom door until I was noticed.

"Dad, please take me to football!" I screamed on the brink of tears. "All my friends are going!"

At the time, my parents were busy trying to provide for us while supporting our extended family in Liberia, most of whom were in the middle of a bloody thirteen-year civil war. The last thing they could have cared about was me wanting to play a sport, especially football; a game which they knew nothing about.

Although they were hesitant, I was very persistent. I knew what I wanted to do and I was relentless. I endlessly begged, bargained, and pleaded with them making it seem like it would be the end of the world if I didn't get to play. I gave them only one option - to take me to my first football registration and sign me up! They saw the love and desire I had for the game. In the fall of

1998, at the age of 10 years old, I began my first year of football. I wasn't doing it just because all my friends were playing. I wasn't forced to play by my father, who had aspired to be a professional athlete, but had a career that was cut short by injury. Both my parents knew nothing about football. It was all on me. I knew that my ultimate success or failure in what I had chosen to do would depend solely on my actions.

My parents sacrificed and worked tirelessly on their jobs. They were barely able to attend any of my games. Early on, I spent many days on the football field feeling like I had no family support. My little league coaches would pick me up for almost every practice and game. On a team full of players whose coaches were their fathers, I found myself wishing my father had the time to at least attend my games. The great performances and big wins were all overshadowed by the fact that my parents were not in attendance. I would always come off the field imagining they would be there, waiting to give me a big hug, and tell me I did a great job. At that young age, their absence was a source of pain, but as I grew to understand the sacrifices they were making, it became a major source of motivation. I can still recall staying up late at night, waiting for my father to come home from a hard day's work. Seeing how hard my parents worked only made me want to work harder.

As the years passed, I didn't realize it, but my sense of self-motivation only became stronger and stronger. I took the fundamental teachings, morals, and examples given to me by my family and applied them to the game of football. They helped me develop a strong work ethic and a "never-quit" attitude. I understood that in order to achieve my dreams, I would have to do things even when I didn't feel like it. I knew I had to perform whether or not I had someone rooting me on. Indirectly, I became my biggest critic. I no longer needed anyone to tell me how good of a job I did. This ability to self-motivate became a good and bad thing. It emerged as such a normal habit that eventually I failed to realize that my family and loved ones did in fact care about my accomplishments. I would forget to invite them to award ceremonies and events thinking that it was no big deal. Eventually, I had to find a happy medium between being self-motivated and allowing the people who cared about me to motivate me and be proud of me as well. It is something they continue to stay on top of and bug me about to this very day.

While playing the game of football, it was pretty easy to distinguish between the kids who were self-motivated and the ones who were only out there because they were forced to play by their parents. I hate to say it, but these were usually the kids who dreaded practice unless there was a pep-rally that day. They would always end up crying and complaining when things didn't go their way. Worst of all, they were the kids who usually gave up when the team was down by only a few scores, seeing no hope of winning. Many people have this same type of attitude and approach in their daily lives. Their only motivation is typically recognition or money. When they don't get what they feel they deserve, they act like those same kids who lacked self-motivation.

Many people end up losing their self-motivation simply because they have been rejected or denied too many times and they would rather not experience that feeling again. This is the same feeling I battled with on a consistent basis when I was released.

After being selected in the third round of the 2010 NFL Draft, I had no idea I would be jobless after just one year. The toughest part of being a free agent was staying motivated when I didn't know what my future held. After getting over the initial disappointment of being released from my team, another mental battle began. I had been training non-stop, trying to keep myself busy. I also knew I had to stay in shape for when a team called me, but as the weeks of the NFL season passed with no calls, it became harder and harder to continue pushing myself. The only thing that forced me to get out of bed in the morning and continue going to the gym to train alone was my self-motivation.

One of the hardest things to do is to stay self-motivated after a letdown of epic proportions, especially when it seems like there is no progress being made. Failures can surely suck the life out of you, but only if you allow it to do so. If the desire of your family and the people in your inner circle for you to succeed outweighs your own desire, there's a pretty good chance you will have a hard time overcoming setbacks. You may have a coach or teacher in your life that can see the potential in you, and in return, is hard on you for reasons you don't understand. In your mind, he or she is getting on your nerves, but in reality, they are only trying to bring out your best. Even though you may not agree with some of the ways they express how much they care for you, these are the individuals who should be commended for trying to create motivation and inspiration in your life. As you transition into the real world, inspirational individuals such as these continually decrease. They will become replaced by people with high expectations and zero tolerance for mistakes; those who will quickly find a replacement for you if they realize you lack the motivation needed in your profession or craft. The parents, teachers, and coaches who were once your authority figures in life become replaced by supervisors and bosses who control your livelihood. Their job depends on your performance, and the last thing they are going to do is hold your hand and tell you that everything will be okay. In the real world, it's survival of the fittest. You must be motivated to work and take care of your responsibilities, no matter if you are sick, tired, or simply don't feel like it.

If you can't find the motivation to work hard and do the right things without someone watching, you're bound to fall short of your full potential. It is important to remember that it all starts with you. There is no formula or magic words that someone can say to change your life. As a free agent, you have to make the conscious decision to go after whatever dream you may have and motivate yourself to the point where you believe the dream is within your reach.

One of the greatest memories I have from playing football at the University of Georgia was my first Georgia vs. Auburn game in 2007. We were in the middle of one of the most exciting seasons ever; coming off a recent win over our rival Florida in Jacksonville. Thousands of fans walked the streets of Athens dressed in all black. Throughout the entire week, there had been an immense amount of anticipation for the game. It was rumored that we would be wearing black jerseys for the first time in

Georgia history and I think I was asked about a million times if the rumors were actually true.

On the day of the game, emotions were sky high as the team went through the Dawg Walk. For those of you who don't know what the Dawg Walk is, imagine a trail with ten to fifteen thousand ecstatic fans aligned on both sides of you, giving you high fives and wishing you luck in your upcoming game. It felt like we were rock stars getting ready for concert!

After we made our way through the crowds, we entered our locker room, and got settled in before everyone began making their way to the showers. We then began our pre-game tradition of praying together as a team with the lights out. The locker room was pitch black. The smell of sweat coursed through the air and the only sounds that could be heard were the voices of young men praising God. The silence broke as soon as the prayer ended. Everyone was as loud and excited as ever. When the lights turned back on, the black jerseys were draped across everyone's seats and the entire team erupted in excitement! I was suddenly knocked on the ground by an offensive linemen jumping around and I cheered even as I lay on the ground. If anyone needed motivation in that moment then there was something seriously wrong with them. As we hit the field, there was nothing anybody had to say or do to get us more motivated and fired up. Our performance spoke for itself, as we won in impressive fashion. To top things off, it was my 19th birthday!

I wanted to tell this story to show how you can be motivated by your environment, the people around you, or even a simple piece of clothing that holds meaning. This type of self-motivation through association is contagious. If you have a hard time motivating yourself, it always helps having external sources that can motivate you. For example, we were already motivated to get the win, but the energy felt from the fans only increased that motivation. I had never heard the stadium so loud before. The motivational spirit of one person can easily trigger and affect the motivation of people around them. One of the best motivational speakers I have been blessed to be around is none other than one of my mentors, Ray Lewis. You can hear the passion he has for what he does in his voice and you can see the dedication in his eyes as he speaks. I hope to one day have that same effect on people; enough to motivate them not only on the field but off the field in their daily lives as well.

I previously mentioned that your environment and other external factors have the ability to motivate you in a positive way, but it can also have the reverse effect. Certain environments and people around you can drain your emotions, body, and spirit. Bad environments and negative influences rob you of the motivation to make the most out of your life. Think about a child who is born in a Third World country, where their parents work for five dollars a day. That is barely enough money to send that child to school. It is not that the parents don't want a better life for their family, but the lack of opportunity and funds force them to only take care of basic needs. In order to help the family, that child must begin working at a young age, putting aside school, sports and any other extracurricular activities that a normal child would get the opportunity to enjoy. It is examples like this fueling the cycle of poverty. There is no motivation for these children to succeed because of their environment and the people around them. Most of the time, this is all they know from birth. Take the same family with the same work ethic, put them in a place with more opportunity, and I guarantee the situation would be completely different.

When looking at self-motivation, you must consider the source of your motivation. Are you motivated by the idea of being able to provide for your family? Are you motivated by a loved one who passed away or are you simply motivated by material gain? You need to ask yourself what drives you and whether this source of motivation is something of substance. If you have a strong belief in your source of motivation, there will almost always be an endless amount of energy giving you the strength to take on whatever task is involved with that belief.

One of my biggest sources of motivation is my beautiful daughter and the day of her birth forever changed my life. It was a beautiful day in Athens, Georgia, on September 23, 2008, when my girlfriend at the time called to inform me she was going into labor. I was in South Carolina with my family and we had just finished up the funeral of my dear aunt who had passed away from breast cancer. I informed my family of what was going on and we quickly made our way down to Athens. I arrived at the hospital, greeted her family, and changed into medical scrubs. After hours of labor, I finally had the opportunity to hold my daughter for the first time. My fatherly instincts turned on instantly. The feeling of love that came over me as my first born child looked into my eyes was unexplainable. It was so intense and something I had never felt before. It was the type of love you could kill for and not even think twice about. At that moment, I made up my mind. My only option was to be successful and I would do everything humanly possible to make sure my daughter was always taken care of.

Since that day, no matter how tough life gets, seeing her makes me want to fight that much harder.

Life takes on a whole new meaning when you know someone is looking for you to provide for them. Suddenly, everything was not about me anymore. The work I did, the sacrifices I made, and the legacy I was trying to build was no longer just for me, but for my future generation. The opportunity to leave something behind for my children to be proud of after I die is another major source of motivation for me. It is always much easier to fight for something when you have something or someone worth fighting for.

When you are in the midst of your crossroad point, spend some time thinking about what drives or motivates you. Ask yourself why you are going to school or work every day. When you are able to find the right type of motivation, you will see that you have more inner strength to endure whatever obstacles come your way. All of the things you are fighting to accomplish will become even more meaningful.

Chapter 4 - Self-Confidence and Determination

As soon as I heard my name called in class, I could feel myself cringe. I always tried to play things off and be the cool kid, but when I opened my mouth to speak in front of everyone, it was a whole different story. My voice would begin to shake, my palms would get sweaty, and my heart would feel as if it were about to burst through my chest. Sound familiar? Self-confidence is the feeling of trust in one's ability, qualities, and judgment.

When I think of this topic, I immediately think of all the times I lacked it, like those times in grade school when I had to stand up in front of the entire class to give a speech or presentation. Similar to many people, standing in front of large crowds used to be one of my biggest fears when I was younger. It wasn't that I couldn't speak or get a point across effectively, It was simply because I lacked the self-confidence needed in that environment. When it came to something that was out of my comfort zone or if I was around people unfamiliar to me, I was totally afraid to express myself. Instead of being focused on the task at hand, my mind was always wondering how people perceived me or what they would say about me.

A lot of people face this same problem at a young age, and in many instances, it is a problem that remains with them their entire lives. Their self-confidence is dependent upon their belief of how people will perceive them and respond to what they say. To some extent, you do have to be mindful of what comes out of your mouth. There are some places where keeping it real and saying whatever comes to your mind just isn't acceptable. It is up to you to find that balance. At the same time, if your self-confidence is solely based upon being accepted by others, you will never truly live or be happy. Some of us only find confidence when surrounded by friends who give us validation, acquaintances that agree with everything we say, or people who we feel are below us. We feel less threatened by them than we would around someone who is more successful, more outgoing, or funnier.

There are a variety of factors that can affect our self-confidence and cause insecurities we don't even recognize. Certain insecurities can stem from what society subliminally tells us about ourselves through the visual media we consume on a daily basis. Whenever you watch television or open up a magazine, everything you believe in or stand for is being challenged without you even knowing it. Often times, the excessive glorification of celebrities and entertainers can influence us to wear certain clothes, style our hair a particular way, or decide what car to drive. Even the most confident person can easily be persuaded by the media and the perceptions that are portrayed. Although this is only one of the many influences that can be associated with negatively affecting our self-confidence, there are some ways to stay above the influence.

I believe one of the most fundamental steps to having self-confidence is to love yourself and simply accept who you are as a person. The beautiful thing about being you is that there is only one! It's so easy to forget that, especially in a world where most of the people who are glorified on a regular basis are athletes and entertainers. It's a shame there always seems to be some type of social pressure for people to be identified within a certain group in order to feel significant. Think about how boring the world would be if we all looked alike and talked the same! Some of the best conversations and experiences I've had in my short life have been with people that were the polar opposite of me. There is beauty in diversity, but a lot of times, we are afraid of what is different. We must realize it is our individual uniqueness that creates value and excitement.

Another factor in obtaining self-confidence is finding your identity. We all put on a different mask depending on our situation or job, but the key is to not let that mask become who we are as human beings.

Figuring out my identity was a major part of my early life. As a young child, being of African descent wasn't something I was always proud of. I knew my culture was not always accepted or received well by my peers. Like other children of African descent, I was called many disparaging names. African booty scratcher and other names were used by ignorant individuals with the sole purpose of degrading where my ancestors and I were from. The ironic part about it was that a lot of the people bullying me looked just like me, which made no sense at all.

It was hard for me to defend my heritage because I was born in America during a Liberian civil war that lasted thirteen years. I was the only person in my family who had never traveled to my home country. The only information I knew about Liberia was from the stories, pictures, and cultural lessons given to me by my parents and grandparents. You can read, hear, and see a million things about a place but there's nothing like actually experiencing it in person. I knew I was of Liberian descent, but I didn't truly understand the importance of what it meant. Because of this, I spent a huge portion of my life trying to be someone other than myself. It wasn't until I was older when I truly became confident in my culture and saw the importance of who I was. I realized that not everyone knows where their ancestors are from and that it was a blessing to know my history. I understood just how unique my story was and how many people could be inspired by it.

I am still amazed by how hard my parents worked to get where they are today and how they overcame the odds against them when it came to living out their dreams in a foreign land. My mother, Josie Curran, came to America on a scholarship to get her master's degree at Emory University in Atlanta, Georgia. She left her home country with nothing other than ten dollars, her hopes, her dreams and a tough work ethic. Can you imagine coming to an entirely new country and having to start a new life at a tough university with no family support? Talk about being totally out of your comfort zone! It takes a large amount of courage and confidence to be able to accomplish such a feat. I had a tough enough time adjusting to my first year at the University of Georgia and I was only forty-five minutes away from home!

As I gained a better understanding of my family, my culture and ultimately myself, my self-confidence truly began to grow. I started to do anything I could to stand out because I knew I wasn't just another person trying to fit in. Instead of shying away from my culture and roots, I embraced it. You must learn to appreciate your foundation, whether it is good or bad, and understand where you come from. Everyone has a unique story and set of circumstances they have to endure in order to get to where they want to be. It is important to realize this and have confidence in your journey and the future journeys that will come your way.

As I grew older, other challenges came along with being an athlete of African descent. It didn't take me long to realize that African-American football players deal with a lot of stereotypes and expectations. When most people looked at me, they only saw a dumb athlete who had nothing going for him. I was expected to talk funny, sag my pants and be the class clown. The people I surrounded myself with wanted me to act a certain way and in order to fit in, I often obliged. These expectations were usually not spoken but indirectly implied. I wasn't a bad kid on the inside but my actions definitely showed otherwise. Throughout middle school, I found myself getting in trouble for the dumbest reasons. I would talk too much or be late to class, and of course, I paid more attention to girls than my academics. I like to refer to this stage in my life as my "knucklehead stage". Like I said, I wasn't a bad kid but boy was I stubborn.

I never realized how brutally honest, straightforward and ignorant we were as young kids in the "knucklehead stage". Speaking correctly, dressing properly and sounding too educated were qualities that many of my peers often looked down upon. Doing such things often resulted in a funny look or an accusation of being "too white". It was never a pleasant feeling hearing people who were supposed to be my friends disparage how I acted.

Now that I look back on this memory, I realize how psychologically damaging it can be to your self-confidence as a child. Being called "white" never strictly referred to color, but was more of a way to call someone weird. As I stated before, people are afraid of what's different. I was afraid of being called this term and did anything possible to straddle the line between acting respectable and still looking cool to my friends. I was trying to live two separate lives and make up for the confidence I lacked in myself by living up to everyone's expectations. For example, I would try to downplay the fact that I was in orchestra because I wanted to be cool. Not that there was anything wrong with being in orchestra, but there weren't too many football players who played the viola.

By the seventh grade, I was constantly meeting with administrators and other figureheads for guidance. I was blessed to have people other than my parents in my life who took a special interest in me. After being drilled time after time and listening to the countless number of lectures, I began to ask myself who I really was. One day, while in the administrator's office, I thought, "Why am I sitting here in trouble?" It was as if a light bulb suddenly turned on in my head. I realized that getting in trouble, being disrespectful and all the other awful things I was doing weren't helping me accomplish anything. For the first time in my life, I understood there was nothing wrong with being a good, well spoken, nicely dressed individual. I use to think my teachers and administrators were against me, but it was at that moment when I realized I was only hurting myself by ignoring their advice. I knew that in order to succeed, I would need to view them as my allies instead of my enemies. I started believing I was a good, intelligent kid and a leader.

The epiphany I had in that office evoked a wave of change

in my life that carried into my eighth grade year when I decided to run for class president. To say that everyone was surprised is an understatement, but I knew I could do it. My self-perception was transformed. I wasn't worried about what others expected from me and was more concerned about what I expected from myself. I wrote a speech and competed against kids that many considered to be more intelligent than me, but I didn't care. All I knew was that I was going to win. My confidence showed as I boldly delivered my speech in front of the entire middle school. A year earlier, I would have never imagined having the ability to stand up in front of a group of people to give a speech, especially the entire school. But on that day, with self-confidence and a little practice, I forced myself to believe I was going to win. I quickly realized that self-confidence was contagious as the belief I had in myself made other people believe in me as well. Once you believe in something so strongly, others have no choice but to follow along and believe in it as well. Many respected public speakers, entertainers and preachers are able to use this ability to get crowds of people to believe in their message.

When it was all said and done, I ended up winning the race for class president. It was a monumental moment in the growth of my self-confidence and I felt like I was on top of the world. I had overcome my knucklehead stage. At least I thought I did.

The growth of my self-confidence came to a screeching halt when I hit the halls of high school. It was a whole new ballgame and I was no longer on top of my own little world. There was a lot more people, a lot more freedom from my parents, and of course, a lot more girls. I was the little guy at the bottom of the totem pole and the stakes were higher than ever before. The pressure to fit in and be cool once again became my main objective. Grades took the backseat and my priorities were all mixed up. My self-confidence became defined by the outfit I was wearing, the girl who said she liked me, and most of all, by doing well on the football field.

Football was my bread and butter. In high school, nothing else in the world mattered except for the events that took place on those precious Friday nights during football season. For a while, it became my identity. My entire self-concept was based on my performance on the field.

Having self-confidence is one of the most crucial attributes of being an athlete, particularly for a football player. How many other professions require you to earn and keep your job by physically outperforming a person who is literally face to face with you? The minute you show weakness, you're finished.

Any good defensive back will quickly tell you the importance of having self-confidence, especially when facing a great quarterback. There may come a time during the course of a game when that player is horribly beaten by a wide-receiver on a play. Part of their job is having the ability to quickly forget about that play and respond to adversity. This requires not only self-confidence but resilience.

As a linebacker, it is our job to call the plays, make adjustments and spearhead the defense. On most teams, the linebacker, usually the Mike (inside) linebacker, is the quarterback of the defense. They must support the run and pass defense. The linebackers tend to be the heart and soul of the defense. In my opinion, which may be just a little biased since I played the position, it is by far the best position on the field. Much like the defensive back, a linebacker cannot be effective without a great deal of self-confidence. They must demand the respect of everyone on the defense with confidence in their voice and body language.

There is no better confidence booster than the feeling you get from winning or accomplishing something great. When I was excelling on the field and in the weight room, I didn't care much about anything else. I loved the sense of satisfaction that came with dominating an offense and being able to completely destroy another man's will. I would hit the weight room for hours, killing myself just so I could see my name on a record board or be given a shirt that showed off my maximum lift.

By my junior year, I had broken a number of records, both on the field and in the weight room, but nothing I accomplished seemed to satisfy me. Eventually, I had to be real with myself and ask, "Is this all I'm good for?" I wondered if anyone could say anything about me as a person aside from the fact that I was a good football player. All my self-confidence was allocated to football and other things that weren't really important when I looked at the grand scheme of things. Take away the title of football player, and I was nothing.

The feeling of nothingness is one of the adverse consequences that can occur when self-confidence is built upon a faulty foundation. Take someone who is driven only by their career. Their main priorities could include being promoted, earning that raise or gaining the respect of colleagues. If their job is taken from them, they may literally feel like their life is over. For some, self-confidence may derive from the clothes they wear. Expensive designer clothing can make them feel like they are on cloud nine. Others attain self-confidence from the car they drive, their house or their significant other. There is nothing at all wrong with striving to be the best at what you do or enjoying nice things, but it can become a problem when the entire foundation of your self-worth is built using things that will be insignificant in the long run.

So much of what you experience when living in the arena of professional sports and entertainment is a facade. Everybody loves you when you can perform, put fans in seats and bring value to a situation. When you are in the spotlight, people will tell you anything you want to hear just so they can be in your inner circle. As the media and different people continually tell you just how good you are, it only becomes a matter of time before you start to develop an inflated sense of self-confidence. It's easy to forget the fact that people don't necessarily like you for who you are as a person but for what you can do for them. You are nothing more than a commodity that can easily be replaced.

I feel sorry for athletes who base their self-confidence solely on their careers. No matter how long or successful a playing career might be, it doesn't last forever. In a profession where money and winning is everything, there isn't much room for things like sympathy and loyalty. Even Michael Jordan, the greatest to have ever played the game of basketball, had to retire at some point. He too had to overcome his transition and be confident enough to move on to the next phase in his life. I had to remind myself of this reality when I became a free agent and remember the foundation of my self-worth. I was forced to look back to the things that once motivated me to live my dream.

Throughout most of my years playing the game of football, I had grown accustomed to being the best player on the field. I worked hard and expected only positive results from my efforts. Never in a million years did I think I would ever be told I wasn't good enough. I found myself sitting alone Sunday after Sunday, wondering why I wasn't playing; asking myself if I still had the abilities that once helped me push pass impossible limits. Like anyone else who has ever been fired or had a shortcoming when pursuing their dreams, I questioned my path. Should I give up or continue to chase my dream?

I could have let becoming a free agent destroy my self-confidence, but I chose to let it empower me instead. I picked myself up, went right back to training and stayed focused on my ultimate goal. I made up my mind that I would continue to work hard at pursuing what I loved to do, even if no one else believed in me. I didn't know when the next opportunity would come but I knew I would be prepared.

For the countless amounts of people who have lost their jobs, businesses or relationships, I encourage you to continue to believe in yourself and never question what is inside of you.

Chapter 5 - Self-Control and Sacrifice

Have you ever been in a situation where you were so angry with someone you were on the cusp of fighting or saying something you would have probably regretted, when a teacher, officer or someone of authority suddenly walked onto the scene? If so, your emotions probably changed immediately. I believe all of us have been or will be in some type of heated situation with a significant other or a friend; the type that has you on the brink of doing or saying something you shouldn't. When that time comes, the amount of self-control you possess will determine whether you act on those emotions or smack yourself back into reality.

Self-control is the ability to control oneself, in particular one's emotions, desires, or the expression of them in one's behavior, especially in difficult situations. This can be one of the hardest abilities to master because of the constant battle within oneself. I am no expert but I feel that as humans, we are naturally conditioned to crave and desire certain things. Unfortunately, many of these things can be bad for us but that doesn't change how much we want them. When trying to better yourself and overcome your crossroad point as a free agent, having self-control is yet another important tool that can set you up for success or ultimately destroy everything you have worked to achieve.

My first lesson on self-control was learning to control the tone of my voice depending on my location. I was constantly reminded to use my inside voice when I was at school and my outside voice when outdoors. I practiced this behavior until it eventually became a learned habit. I was rewarded for good behavior and faced consequences when the rule was broken. This is a simple example that can be applied to many different aspects of our lives right now. There are a variety of situations in everyday life where you must use self-control consciously and subconsciously in order to get the results you want, and there are many different methods you can use to apply self-control in those situations.

Have you ever felt the urge to tell someone how you really feel about them but decided not to because you were afraid of what they might say in return? In that circumstance, fear was used as a type of self-control. Fear or caution can be a good thing when applied with knowledge. There are certain things that require a stronger type of control, especially when you're trying to get where you want to be in life. When it comes to control, patience and timing is everything. If you act on an emotion too soon, you could end up doing or saying something you never intended. On the other hand, if you are too late, you may miss out on huge opportunities. Finding that balance definitely takes time but having the attribute of self-control is crucial in life.

Everyone knows at least one person who had an immense amount of ability but lacked the self-control to support it. They may have been a world class athlete or a very intelligent individual who never lived up to their talents. As a matter of fact, I may be talking about you. It is difficult to witness someone with an amazing God-given gift slowly destroy their opportunities because they have no self-control, especially when everyone else can see their great potential. It's sad but for whatever reason, the individual just can't seem to get it. A great example is someone who lacks the discipline to stay focused in school. They seem mentally capable enough but can't find the drive or ambition to understand what they could accomplish if they just had more self-control and discipline. You can talk to them until you're blue in the face out of the love you have for them, but your advice seems to go in one ear and out the other.

Another example of a distraction that can hold a person back is one I feel everyone can relate to. From my experiences, I've found that the number one catalyst leading to failures and missed opportunities are the use of drugs and alcohol. Using these things may not always hinder someone physically but I have seen an endless amount of drug related incidents that caused many high potential individuals to miss out on a number of opportunities. From suspensions to D.U.I.s to accidents, it seems like there is always someone whose life is destroyed by not using self-control when it comes to drugs and alcohol.

I have never been able to understand how a person can just throw their entire career away for something like drugs. What is so great about something that overshadows all of the hard work, sweat and tears you put into making your dreams a reality? To this day, I just can't make sense of it. Maybe it's because my parents never really did drugs or because I could never stand the smell. I know I am far from perfect but I have no idea what causes people to pick up certain habits and lose control to the point where they are willing to forfeit their potential success.

One of toughest things to experience is losing a loved one from a drug or alcohol related incident or condition that could have been prevented. The graveyard is packed with unfulfilled dreams simply because of bad decisions when it came to drugs and alcohol. In this instance, a lack of self-control can cause pain not only for you, but for the people closest to you.

I have a hard time believing that most people are evil and want to voluntarily hurt others for no reason. Instead, I tend to believe that most negative occurrences directly coincide with a lack of self-control when it comes to anger. Poor anger management is something that hinders many people. There are people sitting in jail right now because of a moment of uncontrolled anger that led them to do things they would have never done in a normal state of mind. I am usually a pretty laid back guy, but there have even been times in my life where I made bad decisions by allowing my emotions to get the best of me.

Everyone has at least one thing that completely sets them off. For me, it's when someone bumps into me and doesn't say "excuse me", or when someone is just rude for no good reason. I can handle a lot, but it's hard to have patience when dealing with blatant disrespect. It is in these moments when I have to use self-control and talk myself out of many disputes. Being able to mentally take a step back and remember how much I have to lose is one of the things that have helped me during numerous conflicts in my life. I could very easily be sitting somewhere in jail right now if it wasn't for that ability. Being an athlete and having everything I do viewed under a microscope also helped as it caused me to look at a lot of things differently. I knew that if I was to ever get into a fight, I would most likely end up on the front page of the sports section. Even if I was just defending myself, I had to learn to walk away in order to protect everything I had spent so many years building.

The hardest lesson I had to learn was how to pick and

choose my battles wisely. I realized the importance of this after seeing certain people in my life who were on top of their respective careers lose everything by committing a single act. I kept in mind that I was not only representing myself, I was representing my family, my school and any organization affiliated with me. I understood that when it came to conflicts, I had much more to lose in the long term than I had to gain in the short term. Having self-control involved making some major sacrifices. The next time you are about to make a bad decision, just thinking about what you will be sacrificing or giving up could change your mind.

In the simplest terms, sacrifice is the ability to give up or get rid of something highly prized or desirable for something that is seen as having more value. This is one attribute that separates those who actually achieve their dreams from those who never move beyond dreaming. It involves self-control and discipline in its highest form. It is always easy for people to talk about the things they want to accomplish in their lives or how they want to make their situation better, but if they fail to think about the sacrifices necessary to achieve their hearts' desires, they will always come up short.

The first thing that comes to mind when discussing our dreams is the type of lifestyles we want to live. When we think about our futures, we often create a perfect world in our minds, totally blocking out anything negative. I remember visiting an elementary school to talk to some kids about pursuing their dreams. It was a class full of excited fourth graders with no idea of what experiences life held for them. One of the first questions I asked was what they wanted to be when they grew up. Their hands quickly rose with the confidence, enthusiasm and innocence that only children can possess. The answers I received were similar to those of many other children around their age, with the dream of being an athlete or some type of entertainer topping the list. The next question I asked was if they knew what sacrifice meant. A few hands raised but I could tell they had no idea what I was talking about.

As I looked deep into the crowd of children, I could see myself and I envisioned how I was at one time. I couldn't help but be reminded of all the hopes and dreams I possessed at their age. I remembered watching my favorite team, the Atlanta Falcons, and thinking of how amazing it would be to play in the NFL. I thought about being on television, buying my mother a house and being able to purchase whatever toy I wanted. Like many people, I was naïve and could only see the surface of my dream. The depth of the trials and adversity I would have to overcome just to make it to that level never once crossed my mind. I knew nothing about being a free agent or the business side of the NFL. All I knew was that you got drafted, signed a major multi-million dollar contract and had fun playing football.

My perception of professional football slowly changed when I got older. As the years passed, the level of competition grew more and more intense. All the teammates I grew up playing with began to quit one by one, year after year. Eventually, I could count the number of guys I'd played with since the pee-wee leagues on one hand. Before I knew it, the game that I loved suddenly stopped being a game. In high school, there were millions of kids like me who were fighting for the chance to earn a college scholarship. In college, there were thousands of players fighting to earn the chance to play in the NFL. In the NFL, there were a couple thousand players fighting to keep their jobs every year. The higher the level of competition meant fewer differences in the level of talent. There were only a few things that could really separate you from the individuals with immeasurable ability. In life, the amount of effort you put forth and how much you are willing to sacrifice can make all the difference in setting yourself apart from others.

Since I was considered an undersized linebacker early in my football career, I quickly realized I had to do everything in my power to set myself apart from the millions of other athletes who possessed the same dreams as me. I had to go over and above in order to make up for my lack of height. Although I was not the tallest, I made sure I was always the strongest pound-for- pound player on any team I played on. If the coach said two-hundred pounds on the bench press, I put on two-hundred and twenty-five pounds. When it came to playing the game, I did everything I could to ensure my technique was as close to perfection as possible. I also did my best to make sure I was always the first player to the ball on every snap, from the first quarter to the last. Because of this, I didn't have to brag about how much better I was than the next player. My film and statistics did all the talking for me.

Setting yourself apart through sacrifice is not only essential in the game of football but in the corporate world as well. There's an endless list of competitive careers out there. Just think about how many doctors, lawyers, insurance agents and car salesmen there are on this earth. The factors that set these individuals apart and help them to differentiate themselves from the pack are the same factors that set me apart when pursuing my career on the field. In any career path you choose, you must realize that in order to truly reach the top, there will always be some type of sacrifice you must make.

In our society, we often look to those successful individuals who are at the pinnacle of their industries and believe they have some type of special ability or talent that makes them different from the norm. It's easier to believe that their success came overnight than to appreciate the amount of sacrifices they had to make in order to be in that position. Occasionally, someone may compliment me for my nice car or ask me how I am able to keep my body built the way it is. After thanking them for the compliment, I immediately think about how they will never know the number of years I had to work in order to get to where I am. All they were able to see in that moment was the finished product; the result of many years of sacrifice. As a free agent, you must always remember that it was the sacrifices you made along the way that got you to your current position and it will be sacrifices that give you the ability to continue moving forward.

Chapter 6 - Success and Fame

When thinking about success and how it pertains to life as a free agent, there are many things that come to mind. The first thing you must figure out is your own view of success. I continually questioned my idea of success as I sat in my room Sunday after Sunday, trying to force myself into not watching any NFL games because of the disappointment I felt from not playing. Once again, I found myself asking if the only thing I was good for was playing the game of football. I wondered if all of the tackles, accolades and newspaper clippings I had accumulated over the years would be what ultimately told the story of whether or not my life was successful.

Some people see success as obtaining enough money in their bank account to give them the ability to have anything they could ever want at their fingertips. Others grade their success in the amount of awards, accolades and high ranking positions they attain. These are all great things to strive for but at what point are you truly considered a success? You might believe that point is reached when you're perceived as being successful by others; however, the individual who is truly successful continues to strive to reach that next level of success. I have heard many people claim that success is not a destination or point that you reach but an ongoing process, and I totally agree.

We all have different goals and ambitions, but at the end of the day, I think it's safe to say we all simply want ourselves and the people we love to have a life of significance. Success is such a hard thing to gauge. You can work your entire life for something, only to look back years down the road and realize you are not happy or fulfilled. Would you call a person who has everything money can buy but has no family or any true people that love them, successful? That's a pretty tough question to answer. There are some individuals that live what others would consider to be a wonderful life, but because of the amount of daily stress they encounter, they can't even sleep at night without taking pills. Think about all of the random suicides, drug overdoses and untimely deaths that have happened to the people in our society who we label as famous or successful. There are a never ending set of examples of people who are perceived to be living the good life but eventually find themselves in a tragic situation.

Success is not always something that can be counted, purchased or given material value. For example; you can buy a house but you can't buy a family; you can buy companionship but you can't buy true love. There were a number of lessons I had to learn before I could understand the true meaning of success. The first lesson was reinforced only a couple months after I was drafted.

It was a rough day of practice with the Titans during my rookie year and I came home exhausted yet excited at the same time. I knew my life was about to change forever, or so I thought it would. This was the day I would receive the first installment of the money from my first NFL contract. I remember being overwhelmed with joy, like a child on Christmas day, as I ran upstairs to get on my laptop. I quickly logged into my online bank account and looked at my checking account to see how much money had been deposited. My jaw fell to the floor as I saw the dramatic change in my bank account. On the inside, for a brief moment, I felt as if I had won the lottery. This was part of the reason why I had chased my dreams so relentlessly, why I had worked so tirelessly since the age of ten and I was finally being rewarded for it. I had spent hours in the weight room, training room and film room for this very moment, and the hard work had paid off, literally. I thought about all the things I could buy and all the places I could go. I remembered how much my family had struggled in the past and knew I would finally be able to provide for them. I felt so much power, like I was suddenly in control of my own destiny. In that instant, I felt like all of my problems were finally solved. I was on an emotional high, and at the age of 22, I truly believed I could finally be called a success story.

Suddenly and without warning, my feeling of accomplishment drifted away and the silence of my townhome became so loud that it overshadowed my excitement. I quickly came back down from my emotional high, realizing I was away from my family and my daughter. The excitement of the money could not fill the emptiness and loneliness I felt from being separated from them. I came to the realization that this would be the tradeoff for the life I had chosen. It was crazy. As a child, all I had dreamed about was becoming a professional football player but I never understood everything that would come with it.

One of the strangest parts of success which most people don't even realize until they are suddenly thrust into that position is that anything of worth comes with a price, a tradeoff or some type of sacrifice. Talk to high ranking individuals from any company and they will probably have a story similar to mine. The more you succeed, the more you tradeoff. Always keep in mind that when much is given, much is expected. In order to live your dreams, sometimes you have to be willing to give up the time put toward the things that matter most in life, including holidays with the family, an important relationship or time with your children. These are memories and experiences in life you can never get back and you must ask yourself if your success is really worth it. I try to never be envious or jealous of anyone in a high position because I can't begin to understand what they had to go through to get to that position or what they will have to endure to maintain that success. I don't know about you, but to me, having a simple life with peace of mind is worth a lot more than a superficial life full of stress. However, the grass is always greener on the other side and it's easy to think that someone else's life is greater than yours when looking in from the outside.

The ability to handle success and fame became another lesson I had to learn. Not only can success be deceiving in terms of what it takes to attain but it can completely change your view of reality. Financial success is a great example of the type of success that can alter our perceptions. It's funny how rapidly we can change into different people depending on the amount of money in our bank account. Even those who come from humble beginnings can have a hard time saying no to things they would normally consider eccentric when they have the ability to afford them.

I will never forget my college years, when the only substantial income I received was from my Pell Grant. The Pell Grant is need-based assistance given to students from low income families. This money, usually only a couple thousand dollars, would have to last me almost an entire semester, but somehow

I would manage to make the money stretch to the point where I could help myself and my family. Fast forward to my rookie year in the League, and I was making more than triple that amount every two weeks. All of the sudden, it seemed like I had a never ending fortune. A couple hundred dollars instantly turned into chump change. I purchased shoes, clothes, furniture and other items I would have never thought about buying in college. Adjusting to financial success was a constant battle that took place in my mind. On one side, I knew I needed to be frugal and make wise financial decisions with my new money. This side of me wanted to save and give money to family or to charity. On the opposite side, there was an entirely different mindset. I would think to myself, "I've worked so hard to be able to do this" or "I deserve this". I used this mentality to justify spending money on things that weren't even on my window shopping list less than a year before. I never had to consider these things during previous struggles in my life. When times were rough, I knew I only had a couple of options if I wanted to survive. But with success came money, with money came more choices and with more choices came more things to consider. I became comfortable with taking more risks when it related to investments, feeling like any choice I made would result in a win. This is one of the reasons why success and fame can be dangerous and twist what you perceive as reality. When things are going great, you can easily believe they will always be that way.

One of the more positive aspects of being a free agent in the NFL arrives after you have proven yourself and shown you can bring value to a team. Like many corporate businesses, an organization will pay large amounts of money to bring in employees who possess a proven track record of being effective and successful at what they do. The key for a free agent in any industry is not allowing improved circumstances to affect your drive. It is important to maintain the same habits that got you to that point. If you lack focus, it becomes easy to relax and lose the hunger for greatness once rewards start flowing your way. Its human nature to feel like you are on top of the world. That feeling of success can trick you into believing you are better than others and can treat them however you want. Sometimes, people begin to ignore those who are seen as failures instead of extending a helping hand or giving them some encouragement to pick them up. For some, success can be just what they need in order to build themselves and others around them, but for others, success can destroy their minds and everything they've worked hard to build.

Not only can success alter what you view as reality, it can change how others perceive you as well. Certain people will begin to see you differently and so-called friends might say you have changed. Others will view you as less of a human being and more like an opportunity that can help them get to the next level. There are people who specialize in taking advantage of others in order to make a living. Like vultures, they smell success and look for any opportunity to prey on those who can bring them monetary value. Every industry has these types of individuals. They are comparable to leeches sucking the life out of you, giving back nothing useful in return. People like this are not always easy to detect. They usually present themselves in the most professional manner and approach with deceitful smiles on their faces, telling you exactly what you want to hear in order to get close to you. No matter how much you are warned, it is easy to fall for their tricks. At times, they will even use the people closest to you in order to gain your trust. As you grow in your success, it is imperative to realize that not everyone who comes around wearing a smile has your best interest at heart.

Through my experience, I have come to truly believe that athletes, entertainers and others in the public eye are some of the most misunderstood people. Just imagine if your life was portrayed through the media on a regular basis. One second, everyone loves you. You're all over the television, the internet and in newspapers. Kids idolize you and the ladies are crazy about you. Now imagine, before you even have time to adjust, the switch turns and people start criticizing you. God forbid you were to go and make a mistake; one that would be sensationalized to the point of making you look like the first person to ever commit a wrongful act. I can almost guarantee that if a film crew followed the average person around for an entire day, there would be more than a few skeletons in their closet they would be afraid to let anyone see. But that doesn't matter in this day and age of technology when pretty much anyone can be a reporter if they want; many of whom are willing to do anything for money, and in a lot of instances, lack any loyalty.

You can do a million great philanthropic things that benefit others and still have one negative incident destroy everything. Nobody wants to hear about the family man who does great things in the community. No, it's the negative stories that drive ratings and grab an audience's attention. This fact brings me to yet another challenging aspect of being successful: expectations.

In life, the more success you gain, the higher everyone's expectations are for you. You are automatically put on a pedestal and held to a standard that most people are never held to. There are way too many examples of great individuals who have fallen as a result of something involving money, a relationship or an act of violence. All of their good works, accomplishments and accolades suddenly become irrelevant. They are remembered in history not for the many exceptional things they accomplished but for the few shortcomings that occurred at some point in their career. In our society, it's no secret that people love negativity much more than positivity. As you become more successful, there will be more people just waiting and itching for you to fail. This brings me to my final point and another obstacle that comes along with success: jealousy.

It is inevitable that you will encounter some form of jealousy or hate when you become successful. Many people will judge you before they ever have had a conversation with you simply because of something they may have heard. Some of these individuals won't accept that you deserve to be in the position you are in, while others will despise your success just because they feel inferior and aren't where they want to be in life. No matter the cause, jealousy is something you will have to deal with on your road to success. If you allow the jealousy of others to affect you, it will slowly but surely bring you down to their level. In order to overcome this challenge, you must remain true to yourself and always remember what made you successful in the first place.

These are just a few of the lessons I had to learn in my

journey of understanding success and fame. Although I wasn't able to play the game I loved after I became a free agent, being away from it allowed me to look at life in a new way. I was able to discover the meaning of true success and wealth. I had poured my entire life into the game of football, fighting hard to establish myself, and at many times, I lost sight of what was most important. In the midst of the disappointment, I looked around and realized how blessed I really was. I finally had the time to spend with my family and my daughter I had once longed for so much. For the first time in my life, I didn't have to stress about performing on the field or worry about who was trying to take my spot. I was at peace. When I looked back on the time I'd spent on the field from high school to the NFL, I realized it wasn't the awards, money or my rare athleticism giving me the feeling of fulfillment that I needed; it was my ability to have a positive effect on others. Even if I was never able to play another down of football, I knew I had been successful because of this. Indirectly, the sacrifices I made on the field allowed me to help my family, my church and my community. I adopted a new sense of gratitude and was thankful for every little thing in my life. Once I had this mindset and began counting my blessings, there was no reason to complain anymore. I knew I would be successful no matter what.

Chapter 7 - Pride and Humility

"Pride goes before destruction, and a haughty spirit before a fall."

This Proverb is something I truly believe in. A person's pride can play a major role in whether they truly achieve their full potential and reach their goals. The amount of pride you possess is yet another attribute that can make a difference in every aspect of your life, no matter what you are trying to accomplish.

What exactly is pride you ask? Well, it can be seen in two different ways. In a more positive sense, pride is defined as a satisfied sense of attachment towards one's own or another's choices and actions, or toward a whole group of people, and is a product of praise, independent self-reflection or a fulfilled feeling of belonging. There is nothing more refreshing than witnessing a person that clearly takes pride in what they do. They might have the task of mopping a set of floors, which may seem insignificant to others, but taking on that task in a positive manner can encourage everyone around them. Everything from the look on their face, their body language and the way they respond to people shows the appreciation they have for their job. Individuals like this don't seem too significant if you only look at their salaries but their value is clearly seen when evaluating the effect that they have on their situation. They are the employees that stick around for the longest and the ones who are never forgotten even after they leave. The pride they take in their jobs and the positive attitude they exude is contagious. No matter what you do in life, whether you are a football player, a teacher, or a janitor, you must take pride in it. You should always appreciate and make the best of your given position. If you find your life is not where you want it to be, try encouraging yourself and taking pride in what you do. Remember, someone is always watching you and you could be one step away from a promotion to that next level.

When thinking about taking pride in one's position, I can't help but reflect on my days playing football before I became a starter. Every team has its starters, its backups and its scout team. The starters get all the action on game day, the interviews after the game and the girls that everyone wants. The backup players only play when the team is up by a lot of points or if there happens to be an injury to a starter. Then there are the scout team players.

The scout team consists of players who are often referred to as tackling dummies or benchwarmers. They are the guys whose names are never called. The only time they ever see the field is if it's towards the end of the game in the final seconds. If someone is placed on the scout team, it is usually not a good thing. It is easy for these players to feel frustrated or believe their role is insignificant. However, the fact of the matter is the scout team is one of the most important and fundamental parts of any team. Every practice, they play the essential role of the upcoming opponent. The better the scout team performs in that role, the more prepared the starters are on game day. The ability to do this requires a group of individuals who go to practice with a chip on their shoulder every single day. They must practice hard day in and day out knowing their names will probably never be mentioned in newspapers or called over the loudspeakers. To avoid letting this fact get the best of them, they have to gain a sense of pride in what they do and understand that they are just as important to the success of the team as the starters. It's definitely a task that is easier said than done, especially in a sport like football where you have to sacrifice your body and push yourself even when you don't feel like it. I will always have a high amount of respect for my teammates who were in this position and never once complained.

Certain people working in the corporate world often face many of the same trials and tribulations a scout team endures in football. Many of them are required to do jobs they view as inferior just so they can provide for themselves and their families. Sometimes you will have to take on certain unwanted positions in life to get where you want to be. When doing this, it is important to remember that even the people who are in the most glamorous situations imaginable had to start somewhere. Your ability to take pride in whatever hand you're dealt can be one of the major factors that allows you to reach your ultimate goal. No matter how low or insignificant you may feel at any given time, you must keep your eyes and heart focused on your final destination.

Taking pride in who you are and what you stand for is another asset that is of the utmost importance on the journey to realizing your dream. You must acknowledge the fact that much like any product sold in stores, you are your own brand. Every time you meet someone for the first time, you give off a certain impression, not unlike the impression given off by a particular car or brand of clothing. For example, if I were to offer you the chance to choose between two cars placed in front of you; one that looked used, dangerous, and costly, and another that represented class, reliability and efficiency, which one would you align yourself with? I'm pretty sure we both know exactly which car you would choose. Now take a moment to think about which one of these cars relates to you as a person. How well do you present your own brand to others around you?

You must have self-pride and demand respect by the way you carry yourself. The impressions you give off can be the difference between being given the opportunity of a lifetime and being passed up by someone half as talented as you. You can have a million degrees or be as qualified as anyone and still find yourself overlooked simply because of the way other people portray you. I don't know about you, but if I were a boss searching for a potential employee, there is no way I would hire anyone who came to an interview looking like they just walked in straight off the streets. When you start taking more pride in yourself, it will be harder for people to take you for granted.

The negative side of pride is referred to as an inflated sense of one's personal status or accomplishments. Certain people are so full of pride they end up becoming too full of themselves. These individuals may seem genuine enough at first, but overtime you can easily point out a prideful spirit or a person who loves themselves a little too much. The worst part is when these prideful beings lack any self-awareness, not realizing how arrogant they truly are. I can't think of how many times I've wanted to look someone in the eye, reveal their own arrogance to them and remind them we are all humans. Having too much pride can make even the most attractive person ugly and the most talented person worthless. Like I've said before, there is nothing wrong with having self-confidence in who you are and what you have accomplished. The problem arises when you allow those feelings to trick you into believing you are better than other people.

Almost every year in sports, there is an example of a dominant team that is defeated by an opponent who had no business beating them. This usually happens when the dominant team lacks the same level of motivation they exhibit in bigger games, believing that their mere presence will result in a victory. This is just one of the many downfalls associated with pride and an inflated sense of self-confidence.

Pride can not only cause you to overlook opponents that have the potential to defeat you, but it can also cause you to overlook the people who can be a blessing in your life. Too much pride can be the worst enemy to someone who is going through a major transition or crossroad. It can cause them to reject the truth and continue on a path to their own destruction. These types of people are often in denial refusing to admit they need the help of others around them. A prideful person can repeatedly be given the best advice but stay mentally trapped in their own little world. They end up missing out on great opportunities to improve their talents and abilities because they reject any coaching or mentoring. In time, the people who originally wanted to help that individual may be pushed away because they are tired of dealing with a know-it-all attitude.

It's always sad to witness a person let their position in life deceive them into thinking they are better than others. Because of the way life works, it is important for you to control your sense of pride. We are all in different seasons of our lives and just because things are sunny today, there is no guarantee there won't be rainy days ahead. If you are in a high position you should make a conscious effort to be humble, treat others around you with respect and not look down on them. You may be on top of the world today but things can quickly change and those same people might just be the ones who will help pick you up if you fall. In order to make it through the numerous crossroads in life, you must completely reject the inflated sense of confidence that can come from pride and adopt an attitude of humility.

Humility is one of the most important attributes that will aid you in your time of growth. Remember, pride and arrogance comes before destruction and humility comes before honor. If pride is the lock that closes doors of opportunity, humility is the key that opens the door of infinite personal growth. Humility refers to a modest or low view of one's own importance and it is crucial you develop this trait on your journey to discovering who you are as a person.

Being humble involves having maturity as well as wisdom. These intangible assets do not just come overnight but are built by the constant application of self-awareness in your surroundings. Having self-confidence in life is definitely important, but this attribute becomes even more valuable when you add humility. It takes a wise and humble person to realize their intelligence, but understand that they will still learn something new every day. No matter how smart you may think you are there is always someone who will know more about certain things. None of us are all-knowing. The ability to take the advice of family, close friends and others who have your best interests at heart will help you avoid many pitfalls and disappointments.

Humility is especially important when you realize your talent in life. It forces you to continually work at your craft because you know there is always someone else who has the same amount of potential as you. As I stated earlier in this book, I have been playing the game of football for thirteen years but I still understand there are many improvements that must be made to my game. No matter how well versed you may become at your craft you must realize there is always something more that can be done to take you to the next level. In sports and business, the difference between good and great is miniscule. An individual possessing too much pride will likely allow their confidence to subdue their work ethic, while the humble individual will usually maintain the hunger that led to their success.

Those who possess humility are always coachable and endlessly work to improve their skills no matter how flawless. They never allow themselves to become comfortable or complacent.

I was eighteen years old the first time I met another one of my future mentors, Stevie Baggs. I happened to be training at my alma mater, Brookwood High School, on the same day as him. It was Spring Semester of my senior year and I was coming off one of my best seasons of high school football. I had already committed to my future college, the University of Georgia, and the only thing on my mind was being prepared for the journey that lay ahead of me in Athens. I had already achieved a lot in my high school career. Along with other accolades I'd received, I was my school's all-time leading tackler and had won the Georgia

Weightlifting competition for my weight class; but I knew that almost every player in college would be an exceptional athlete as well. I had to set myself apart but I didn't quite know how I would do it.

Just as I was midway through my training session, I noticed a man doing linebacker drills on the main field; a man who looked like an older version of me. I observed him from afar; taking mental notes of his technique and the drills he did. By the look of him, I knew there was no way he could be a high school player. I saw myself one day becoming the figure I saw and quickly approached him for advice.

"Excuse me," I said as I walked onto the football field where he had the cones lined up for his drills. "I saw you doing linebacker drills. Could you show me some stuff?"

I thought he would surely blow me off, but to my surprise, he took time to give me some advice. After speaking with him, I learned he played for the Canadian Football League and he wasted no time in showing me some of the drills and techniques that had helped him on the professional level. We instantly became great friends and still are to this day. I had no idea asking him that one question would have had such a monumental effect on my life, and it was nothing other than humility that drove me to approach him and ask for his advice. Most people don't realize that if you simply humble yourself and ask for help many of the individuals who seem impossible to reach would be more than happy to help you. Sure, there is a chance you may get rejected but so what? All it takes is one "yes" to change your life. No matter what industry you are in, admitting you need help can play a major role in your success.

Although humility is a great attribute to possess, too much of anything can be dangerous. As I stated in the previous chapter, there are a number of individuals who will take advantage of the humble, respectful and loyal people of the world. If you don't place enough value in yourself and the skills you possess, people will walk all over you. You must have the pride to stand up for yourself without burning any bridges. If you notice yourself becoming too prideful, just think back to the times in your life when you have failed. In that moment, you will find the necessary balance of pride and humility inside of you.

Chapter 8 - Failures

I looked up at the scoreboard as the clock wound down and all I could think about was how we should have and could have won the game. Millions of thoughts ran through my head. My body ached with pain, was covered in sweat and I had given it my all. Even though I knew I had left everything on the field as I walked back to the locker room, it did nothing to bring me satisfaction when the reality of defeat set in. The feeling in my stomach was similar to the sour stomach feeling I got from food poisoning and it only got worse.

Going into the final game of my junior year at Brookwood High School, we were undefeated, and it was one of the best teams I had ever been a part of. It could have been the game that solidified our season, but we lost.

There were a million questions racing through my head as the clock hit zero. Had everything we worked for been in vain? Was our game plan as good as we thought it was? Did we practice hard enough that week? Who was to blame for our loss? Did we have the right personnel? These are some of the same thoughts that often accompany failure in any avenue of life. It's always hard to perfectly describe success because everyone sees it in a different way. At the same time, everyone has a pretty similar view of failure, which is the inability to achieve a goal or reach your fullest potential.

Knowing you have failed at something is a miserable feeling. It doesn't matter if it's a failed test or failed relationship; it always leaves the same feeling of incompetence, especially if you know you gave your best effort. It can feel like a punch in the stomach; an unbearable pain that will linger if you allow it.

As a free agent in the midst of your transition, learning how to deal with and overcome failure is another vital asset that must be developed in order to rise above the variety of circumstances you will face.

Like most people, my first feelings of failure came in my early childhood years. It was something as simple as getting an answer wrong when called upon in class. I hated not being right. My self-esteem would be totally shot if I got an answer wrong numerous times. I wouldn't even want to make another attempt to answer a question for the very fear I would be wrong even if I knew the answer was right. It's easy to let our shortcomings create mental walls that keep us from taking chances and cause us to worry about failures that may or may not ever happen. There are many people in this world who are still suffering from depression due to the failures they experienced early in their lives. They can't seem to get over or forgive themselves for these failures. You can see it in their eyes, hear it in their voice and even see it in their body language. They let that one failure consume them until it takes over every single part of their life. Some people stop pursuing their dream career because they suffered a setback in the business world, while others let the heartbreak felt from a failed relationship change their outlook on finding love. The examples are endless, but at some point, everyone will experience a type of failure or setback.

I can go on and on about the times I've failed on the football field and in life. It has been these same failures that have aided me in becoming the man I am today. For example, there have been a number of instances when someone takes a look at my body and then asks how strong I actually am. They're amazed when I tell them my maximum lifts: 470 pounds on bench, 615 on squat, and 350 on power cleans. What they don't realize is how many times I had to fail in order to get these numbers and the years of training it required. I had to fail, learn why I was failing and then change my habits in order to improve my technique little by little. One thing was for sure, I had to get out of my comfort zone and push my body beyond its limits. Mentally, I had to picture myself lifting weights that were twice my body weight. Results didn't come overnight. There were days when I would leave the gym barely able to walk. There were times I didn't want to continue on and I often questioned whether all my efforts would lead to positive results. Through these different experiences, my body was becoming physically and mentally stronger. Each failed attempt became something for me to build on.

Failure can be one of the greatest tools for growth, but if you never appreciate the lessons that failure brings, it will consume you and restrict you from reaching your God given potential. My experience with failures in the weight room is no different from the pathologist trying to find a cure for a disease. They must conduct a number of experiments, slightly changing the variables until the right combination is discovered. Entrepreneurs trying to create a new product can have a similar experience as they work days and nights trying to come up with the next big idea. In the music industry, there are millions of bands and artists around the world playing countless shows at local bars, working odd jobs and going through adverse conditions, just to have the opportunity to one day be a household name. In most industries, only a small amount of free agents will make it all the way to the top.

When reminiscing on the topic of failures, I am reminded of a quote by the late Zig Ziglar which states: "We should get excited about difficulties in our life because that develops character, character develops persistence, persistence develops performance, and you start putting all those things together. It's the result of the difficulties we face." Sometimes the best lessons are taught through pain and disappointment. When things are going well, it becomes easy to get complacent and comfortable. It's in our nature to ignore certain details when there is success. Failure forces you to evaluate everything. It's that rude reality check that comes every so often, causing you to regain your focus and become aware of everything that affects you. Many times, it gives you an ultimatum: Either continue on the same road with the same results or take a detour that will improve your chances of success.

When it comes to accomplishing something great, something that a lot of people will never have the chance to accomplish, you must accept the fact that nothing happens overnight and have the ability to turn setbacks and disappointments into opportunities that can display greatness. There were many times on the field when I completely blew a play and was embarrassed by my opponent. I had two choices: I could either dwell negatively on that play or shake it off and respond. If I chose to dwell, things would only get worse. Such is life. It's always easy for someone to keep a smile when everything is going well, but what happens when you are faced with failure? How you respond to failure is what reveals your true character. Are you the type of person who starts to point fingers? Are you the person who completely falls apart when obstacles arise? The different ways you react to failure can quickly reveal what type of person you are.

One of the best tools used to overcome failure is resilience, or the ability to bounce back, and there are only a few ways to build this attribute. You'll never know what truly lies within yourself until you go through some type of adversity and are forced with a choice to either lie down or fight back. Possessing resilience does not guard against the pain and disappointment of failing but it enables you to realize the pain is only temporary and you aren't a failure. Like a boxer in a fight, there are times when life will straight-up knock your lights out, and most of the time, you won't even see it coming. However, the only way you will lose is if you stay on the ground. You must have the ability to get back up, dust yourself off and keep on moving.

No matter how painful and disappointing the setback may seem, there is no such thing as a complete loss when experiencing failure. Each time you fail, you become stronger and wiser in the process. I don't know about you, but I get pretty fired up when I face a challenge, or when someone tells me I'm not good enough to do something. Many of the most successful people are in their respective positions because of the failures they experienced and learned from early in life. Albert Einstein was expelled from school; Thomas Edison made one-thousand unsuccessful attempts when inventing the light bulb; Bill Gates dropped out of college, and Oprah was fired as a television reporter after being labeled "unfit for TV". You could find a million success stories that benefited from failure early on.

Life has a funny way of coming full circle. No matter how confusing it may seem at times, everything eventually makes sense. There are many opportunities that can be created through failure if you possess the right attitude. I would have never started writing this book if I hadn't been cut by the Tennessee Titans. Instead of drowning myself in depression, I decided to turn my downfall into an opportunity to inspire those who have been or will be in a situation similar to mine. The next time you are faced with failure, I challenge you to find the opportunity to bounce back and turn your disappointing setback into a joyous comeback!

Chapter 9 - Giving Back

It was the year 2000 and with it came one of the coldest winters in recent memory. For the first time in my life, we had been hit by a major ice storm in Georgia. It completely knocked out the electricity as well as other normal luxuries we were well accustomed to. We were always excited at the possibility of snow in Georgia because just one inch meant no school, but the ice storm was a completely different story. When I looked outside my window, I saw the fallen trees, damaged telephone poles and torn power lines that filled the streets. Making the situation even worse, my father had recently lost his shoe repair business and was going through the mental struggle of not being able to provide for our family for the first time. In addition, my mother was recovering from surgery after getting fibroids removed from her uterus, resulting in complications that almost took her life. All I could do was watch helplessly as she lay in bed fighting for her life. For many years before this struggle, both of my parents had worked tirelessly to help their families during the thirteen year war in Liberia; sending money, clothes and whatever resources they could gather. Due to unfortunate circumstances, things had drastically changed and suddenly we became the ones who were in need of assistance.

Christmas time was approaching but presents, delicious food and happy times were the last things on my mind. Actually, at times, I dreamt of getting the newest video game or some new clothes but I wouldn't have dared to ask my mother for anything. I knew we wouldn't be able to afford it and I accepted the fact that what mattered most was making it through this time. We were never rich but we always managed to get by, and the love and unity we had for each other always kept us strong. However, this was one of the lowest points for our family and without the support from certain people who took a special interest in my life, I could have easily slipped into a major depression.

One afternoon during the storm, I heard the doorbell ring. As I ran and opened the door, I saw my little league coach's wife, Mrs. Benton, and her son J.T. holding bags of Christmas presents and gift certificates for groceries! Families from my little league team had somehow heard about our struggles and came together to offer us support. Like angels sent from God Himself, they arrived just in time to give us a hand when we needed it most. Suddenly, we had hope! What could have been one of the worst holidays imaginable became one of the best memories of my life because of people who were willing to offer us help when we were down on our luck. They didn't do it for recognition, to get anything in return or because I was a good football player. They simply acted out of the kindness of their hearts.

When I think about the importance of giving back, I can't help but to immediately reflect on my childhood and the countless people that offered me support. I would have never made it where I am today if it weren't for others taking a special interest in my life and wanting me to succeed. None of us are self-made and none of us magically arrive at our aspired destination without some type of help, recommendation or assistance along the way. Whether it's family, a teacher or a coach, we all have someone or something in our lives that inspires us. I believe you should always give back and not forget about where you come from. It's also important to remember the people who were there for you along the way.

No matter where you are in life, free agent or not, we all give and receive a certain amount of influence. The influence we give should not be used to display our greatness but to have a positive impact on others. No matter what you do in your own life, there is always potential to have an effect on someone else's life. The ability to use your blessings, gifts and talents to help others is one of the best feelings in the world. Once you can find a way to successfully influence others, your life will become that much more fulfilling. Being part of something bigger than yourself can help you transcend your job title and become an agent of change.

Realistically, there are roles in society that have more influence than others. Many times, a child will have trouble listening to a parent or teacher, but when their favorite athlete takes the time to talk to them, they're all ears. This is one of the things I love the most about being a professional athlete. My greatest enjoyment doesn't come from hitting someone full speed or earning tons of money and fame; it lies within the platform of influence it provides. Every day, I come in contact with people, especially children, who are experiencing issues I can't even fathom. They may be dealing with a divorce, the loss of a loved one or a number of other struggles in life. It's an amazing feeling knowing I can make a difference in their day just by speaking to them! After all of the influence given by my teachers, coaches and mentors that helped turn me into the man I am today, there is no way I could ever turn my back on others seeking that same kind of influence in their lives.

One of my biggest childhood dreams was to make it to the NFL so I could take my entire family back home to visit Liberia. After years of playing football, my hard work and relentless determination finally paid off and I was able to turn that dream into a reality. My parents, who had been away from Liberia for over twenty years, had sacrificed so much for me throughout my life and the fulfillment I received from helping them return to their beloved home was spectacular.

It was a grueling trip that spanned from Atlanta to Brussels, Belgium. After many hours of travel and a long layover, the captain finally came over the loudspeaker to make an announcement: "Please return to your seats as we are beginning to make our initial decent. We will be arriving in Liberia shortly." The words coming from the intercom didn't seem real and my eyes immediately shot out the window. As the clouds cleared, I was able to take in the breathtaking view of the African Coast.

While gazing out of the window in amazement, my mind drifted back to all the memories I had growing up and hearing stories about Liberia. Everything I knew about my country had come from my family. When my grandparents came to America they would bring pictures, clothes and foods that were authentically made in Liberia. I was raised with Liberian morals, ate Liberian food and even went to a church full of mainly Liberians. Although a huge part of my life was centered on my culture, not being able to experience my home country firsthand left a hole inside of me. Now, looking over Liberia, I knew that was all about to change.

Our emotions ran high as we gradually descended towards

the country. I turned to my two sisters, Joan and Musu, and noticed their faces were full with tears of joy. Once I turned back to my window, all I could see was the beautiful miles of coastline and green vegetation. We finally landed and began to make our way off the plane. I felt like I was in a dream. I was so excited to be there I hugged the entire Liberian air traffic control crew as if they were part of my family, even getting my picture taken with them! A wave of emotions came over me as I took in the entire experience. For the first time, I felt like I was somewhere I belonged; I felt at home.

A big part of my trip, aside from tracing my roots and taking my family back home, would be to find ways to give back to the country. As I left the airport, I met a variety of children, media crews and even family I'd never seen before. Even though I was not born in Liberia, the people of the country seemed to embrace me because I cared enough to visit and give back. Many of the people were also proud and excited to see one of the few Liberian NFL players. After a couple of interviews talking about my first time being in Liberia and my initiative of wanting to help the country, I was greeted by my grandmother and other relatives. We exchanged smiles and hugs before making our way to my grandfather's house for a major celebration. As I rode through the city, I could see the damage that had been done by the civil war, but at the same time I noticed the development that was starting to take place. I couldn't wait to do my part to help.

After spending the first couple days in the capital city of Monrovia seeing family, visiting officials from the government and nonprofit sector, and checking out different attractions, we finally made our way to Gbarnga. The city was the capital of Bong

County, Liberia where my mother's village was located. Along the way, we passed the high school where my parents met for the first time, as well as their college. However, I was concerned as I watched my parents' faces turn from happy and excited to sad and disappointed. The memories they once had of Liberia were nowhere to be found.

"This use to be beautiful," said my mother. My father replied in turn, "The war has destroyed our country."

Thankfully, their feelings of disappointment quickly drifted away as we approached my mother's village. I could see a large crowd of people gathering from afar, and as we moved closer, the crowd began marching towards us. They marched together in unity; throwing rice and dancing in the streets. My mother then informed me the crowd full of nearly one hundred and fifty people was my family! The celebration only grew as we got out of the car. There was hugging, smiling and years of catching up that would follow. We soon marched through the town up to my grandfather's house. I was able to see where my mother was born, where my great grandparents were buried and learn about the entire history of my family. It was an amazing moment in my life.

In the middle of all the excitement, I noticed a group of kids playing an intense soccer game. I walked toward them, noticing they wore their everyday clothes for uniforms and flip- flops for cleats. The goalie had rubber latex gloves as his only defense equipment. I immediately realized how blessed I was to have been given the opportunity to use great equipment, train at state-of-the-art facilities and obtain a college education. As I watched them play with excitement, a certain reality set in. I knew no matter how talented these kids became, very few of them would ever be discovered or have the chance to pursue their dreams simply because of their circumstances. A feeling of thankfulness came over me, followed by a feeling of sorrow for them. I wished there was more I could do, but all I could do in that moment was promise them I would return.

Once the celebration at my mother's village finished, we made our way to my father's village. It was even deeper into the countryside and terrible road conditions turned what should have been a two hour trip into an elongated journey. Occasionally, we would pass by kids with no transportation who were forced to walk miles upon miles just to attend school, which made our long ride not seem so bad.

We arrived at my father's city of Zorzor in Lofa County, Liberia, which was one of the most devastated cities as a result of the war. I had been anticipating seeing my grandmother's house, but that anticipation was soon overshadowed by the that fact it had been burned to the ground. I could only leave it up to my imagination to envision the life my father had lived.

The beauty of Liberia was often clouded by its poverty. Like most third world countries, Liberia has no middle class. There are members of the upper-class who are better off than a lot of Americans, and a lower class of people living in unbelievably poor conditions. As I looked around, I couldn't help but to envision the day when I could make things better for the country and the lives of its people. I knew I was only one man, but it didn't matter. There were so many things I could do to give back. I realized I could be a positive agent of change for them. I didn't want recognition or anything in return. I simply wanted to help them out of the kindness of my heart. Suddenly, the game of football meant so much more. I was no longer just playing for myself and my family. I was playing for the children in those remote Liberian villages who would never be discovered; for the people who needed an opportunity that would bring them the hope needed to continue on!

I returned from Liberia with a new sense of gratitude and appreciation for every little thing in my life. The trip had completely changed me by revealing what held true importance. There is someone in your life who will be affected by the sacrifices you make. They will look to you to be inspired and will find hope because of something you do. When you eventually make it through your time of transition as a free agent, it is my hope you will give them the inspiration they are seeking.

Chapter 10 - The Importance of Relationships, Family, and Faith

I was traveling back to my townhouse in Nashville after several months of being home. Not too far behind me was my father, who followed in a newly rented U-Haul truck. The football season was over and with no calls from a new team, I had no choice but to move all of my possessions back to my parents' place where it all began.

It had been only two years since I moved into the townhome; excited at the prospect of beginning what I had hoped would be an amazing NFL career. The memory of being drafted, moving into my first place and getting my first signing bonus was still fresh in my mind as I walked through my former home. The reality of being a free agent sunk in even deeper as I began packing. All the feelings of accomplishment had now transformed into feelings of disappointment. I tried to console myself with positive thoughts: "At least you made it to the NFL. How many people can say they accomplished that? You got to see and experience things that most people never will."

I continued to try and encourage myself as I moved my possessions to the U-Haul truck waiting outside but thinking about the work I had put in to earn that townhouse and the memories I had created while I was there made it so much harder to leave. When I first arrived in Nashville, I barely had anything besides my clothes, a few electronics and my keyboard. Now it took a U-Haul truck to transport all of the possessions I had obtained. After hours of hard work, we packed the last things into the truck and I said my final goodbyes as we made our journey back home.

A million different emotions and thoughts ran through my

head as we traveled back to Georgia. I had feelings of hope, doubt, fear and optimism all mixed into one, but there was another distinct thought that came to my mind. It arose when I caught the view of my dad driving the U-Haul truck in the rear-view mirror and it remained there like a splinter in my head: What would happen to all of the things in that truck if I were to die tomorrow? Would it be given to my cousins? Would it collect dust or be sold on eBay? I wanted to think it would be sent to people who actually needed it.

There is no telling what will happen to any of our material possessions when we pass, but one thing is for sure, we can't take any of it with us. Once you take your last breath material things become of no value. No man or woman, no matter how rich, can purchase more time on this earth. The most important things in life are not found in the worldly possessions you acquire, but through personal relationships, family and faith.

The importance of your relationships, your family and your faith cannot be understated. They will be essential aspects helping you on your journey to realize you dreams. The success of a variety of individuals has been based on their relationships, their family life and their faith. Take a moment to look at who a person associates themselves with, the past and current state of their family life and their core beliefs. You can probably make a pretty accurate guess on where they are headed in life based off of these factors. You must take these topics into consideration when thinking about getting through times of adversity and change. At least one of these aspects will play a crucial role at each point of your transition. No matter how many wins I've had, tackles I've made or awards I've won, once I am unable to produce on the field, I will be replaced by a younger, more talented and healthier player. Similarly, there may come a time when you are replaced at your job. This is why when you are finding yourself as a free agent, it is important to realize there are things in life that are bigger than your job title. I love being a professional athlete but I understand that once the crowds dissipate, the cheers stop, and the money ends, it will be my relationships, family, and faith that matter the most.

When I reflect on relationships, I think about the billions of people in this world. Do you realize how many people you come in contact with on any given day? Out of all these people, have you ever asked yourself why only a certain number of them actually become a part of your life? You could meet someone randomly at a bus stop, in class or through a mutual friend, but there is no way any meeting can be based on chance. I believe all relationships in life, from the beginning to the end, are there for a reason. Some relationships may be long, others may be short, while there will be a few that come and go over the years. Either way, your relationships with others will play a crucial role in your life and can sometimes determine whether or not you achieve your dreams.

It is important to realize you will attract certain people to your life based on your attitude, your habits and the way you carry yourself. A quote by author Thomas Dreier states: "The world is a great mirror. It reflects back to you what you are. If you love, if you are friendly, if you are helpful, the world will prove to be loving and friendly and helpful in return. The world is what you are." Realizing this simple truth will help you no matter what phase of life you encounter. I've been asked numerous times if it is hard to stay on track as a professional athlete because of the number of distractions we have to deal with on a regular basis. I can honestly say that negative issues only arise when I put myself in negative environments and around the people who are attracted to those environments. In simple terms, if you go looking for trouble, you're going to find it. It all comes back to you. On the other hand, when you mentally focus on your goals, doing your best to fulfill the requirements needed to achieve them, you will attract individuals that will help you along the way.

Although there are many people that will come into your life, it is always your choice to allow them to remain in it. Who you are surrounded by can make or break you. People can inspire you to do good deeds or pressure you into doing things you will regret. There is no way you can achieve what you want in life without aligning yourself with individuals who have your same beliefs. You can't aspire to be a professional athlete, a doctor or a lawyer and spend most of your days with a group of drug dealers. It doesn't make sense. There will always be a conflict of interests when dealing with people who have a completely different life agenda.

There were a number of individuals I chose to surround myself with on my journey. They were the ones who inspired me by believing in me when it came to the game of football. I remember attending the Infinity Football Academy for the first time at the age of thirteen years old. It was run by guys like Stacey Bailey, Floyd Hodge and many other former Atlanta Falcons players. I was in my first year of high school and I was on a mission to become the best linebacker possible with a dream of playing forty-five minutes down the road at the University of

Georgia. My position coach at the academy saw my potential and offered me many words of encouragement and advice. I didn't fully appreciate his presence and understand the importance of the relationship we had formed until years down the road.

When my sophomore year of high school ended, I began to receive interest from different colleges. I ended the season with 145 tackles, along with several tackles for loss and a few interceptions. However, instead of my statistics being the point of discussion, my height became a major factor. At five foot ten, the so-called experts began to label me as an undersized linebacker. No matter how many tackles I made per game, how strong I became in the weight room or how good of a kid I was off the field, it seemed like everything came back to my height.

In my junior season, I consistently made at least fifteen tackles a game, ending the year with 198. I continued to hear the critics talk about my size, but at the same time, I began drawing comparisons to a former Falcons player, Jessie Tuggle. I started hearing people compare me to Jessie so much I finally decided to learn about the man myself. After searching on the internet, I finally came across his picture. My mind immediately flashed back to the times I had spent at the Infinity Football Academy and I quickly realized he was in fact the position coach that had offered me so much encouragement a few years earlier!

Jessie Tuggle is a former linebacker who played for the Atlanta Falcons. He was also inducted into the College Football Hall of Fame, a five-time Pro Bowler and was considered an undersized linebacker just like me. He wasn't recruited by any major colleges but made the best of his opportunities at Division-II Valdosta State. He would go on to silence any doubters by playing fourteen years in the NFL. Not only was he a great football player, he was seen as a leader with a great reputation and was known for his character on and off the field. I decided to reach out to him. If he was able to accomplish so much after being doubted by so many, then maybe there was a chance I could do the same thing.

I was surprised to hear he remembered me and was keeping up with my progress. He then continued where he left off, giving me more advice and showing me techniques that helped him become great in spite of his perceived weaknesses. Despite going through high school and college continually hearing about my stature, I was confident because I knew I wasn't the first undersized linebacker to play the game. I acknowledged that greatness was possible regardless of my physical limitations, and that I could lessen any weaknesses by maximizing my strengths.

No matter what career you dream of pursuing, always remember to form relationships with those who are already successful in that career and gain knowledge from their experiences. If you want to be a surgeon, try to align yourself with a successful one and find out what it took for them to achieve that success. The key word is successful. Those who are successful usually want to see others become successful as well. They won't have any ulterior motives since they have already achieved their goals. Others may be prone to tell you that whatever you are trying to accomplish is impossible, especially if you are trying to achieve something that has never been done before.

The most important aspect of any relationship is the way it is built and nurtured. Respecting and treating every person equally is something that has helped me every step of the way.

You never know who could help you along your journey just because of the way you treated them in the past. There are so many people who have been awarded their current positions simply because others spoke highly of them and recommended them for that job. At the same time, people have missed out on opportunities because no one was willing to speak up for them. You must build and nurture the relationships you have in your life, even with those who could be considered your enemies. It is important not to burn any bridges with other people while on your journey to success. It was this lesson that paid many dividends as I went through my job interview for the NFL.

The NFL Combine is what those in the world of football refer to as the biggest job interview. Although many people get to see the physical evaluations that take place, there are many other tests that are never heard about. During the NFL Combine you are evaluated from head to toe, kind of like a lab rat. It starts with medical testing, followed by mental tests and ends with the physical evaluations that are seen on television. At the end of each day, you are required to have informal and formal meetings with certain teams that are interested in acquiring your services. During an informal meeting, you are put in a large room full of different teams who will ask you a couple of questions to get a better feel for you. A formal meeting is a totally different story.

A formal meeting begins by walking into a room and sitting down in front of some very important people. From your left to your right is the general manager, head coach, position coaches and player development personnel from a particular team and they are looking straight at you. You are officially on the hot seat. When a team is getting ready make a major investment in you, they want to know everything about you, including your past. Not only will they do a background check but they will talk to others who have had any type of relationship with you. Many players find their draft stock falling because of what others say about them. Choices they made in the past end up having a negative effect on their future. These people forgot to be respectful, forgot to respond to others when they are called and forgot to nurture their relationships. These same individuals become ashamed when their circumstances change and they realize that nobody is in their corner to help them.

This type of situation highlights why it is so important to maintain a strong relationship and reputation with those around you. Having strong relationships will get you past many doors that may be shut otherwise. Some of the most successful businesses in any industry are one's that understand the importance of taking care of relationships. Like athletes in the sporting world, companies must compete with each other when offering their services to potential clients, and the success or failure of any given company depends on the reputation they build with their customers. Everything comes back to relationships when it's all said and done. It doesn't matter if you are the world's best hair dresser or insurance salesmen, the more likable you are and the better you treat others, the better your business will be. Try not to get too caught up in making profits and remember if you take care of your relationships by focusing on loyalty and fairness, the money will come.

I can't talk about relationships without discussing family. Family will always be there for you, even when everything else fails. Keeping them close is crucial, especially when going through times of uncertainty and major changes. I was blessed to be raised in a family where I had both of my parents. Of course, things were far from perfect. They argued, talked about leaving each other and still have many disagreements to this day. They enjoyed the good times and fought through the bad times. I've realized just how rare this is as I have grown older. I am always wishing I could find someone who would want to spend the rest of their lives with me and I'm hoping to have a marriage half as good as my parents'. I don't know if it's our culture, our prayers or the simple comfort they have with each other that has kept them together all these years, but I believe their relationship has had a major effect on my life. I never had to split time or choose between my parents and I never had to experience my mother or father using me as leverage against each other. Both my parents worked tirelessly, but at the end of the day, we were happy. The lessons and morals my family taught me have stood the test of time, helping me to become the man I am today. Being respectful, being humble, staying out of trouble and always working hard were things my family not only talked about but demonstrated through their actions. I had many opportunities to go against what my parents taught me and make the wrong decisions, but almost every time, I was able to stay on the right track. When I became a free agent, it was these same lessons that kept me mentally stable when I could have very easily gotten discouraged.

A family does not always have to be blood related. When I think about other families I have been blessed to be a part of, my little league football team is the first thing that comes to mind. I was fortunate to play on a team that stayed together for seven years. We were called Benton's Broncos. Out of all the years I have played the game of football, these were some of my favorite with some of the best memories. Football was nothing but a fun game back then. Since I was the youngest child and the only boy in my family, being a part of this team was like having my own special group of brothers. Over the years, we compiled a winning record of 61-6, but our bond was not solely based on winning games. The most important bond we had was our ability to overcome the many obstacles in our way by depending on each other. The life lessons we learned together through the game of football could never be replaced. I can still remember our motto to this day: "A quitter never wins, and a winner never quits!" Little league was when I learned to never give up and always try my best. After a loss, our coach, Ronnie Benton, would sit us down and challenge us to go home, look ourselves in the mirror and decide what we wanted for the rest of our season. Years later, as a free agent, I found myself staring at my reflection in the mirror many times, asking the same question about what I wanted in my life.

Through the waves of success and failure, triumphs and disappointments and breakthroughs and setbacks that took place in my life, I was anchored by my faith in my Lord and Savior Jesus Christ. Depending on your religion, faith is the belief that there is a God, Gods, or in the doctrines or teachings of a religion. Faith is also trusting or believing in something without any proof of its existence. I couldn't quite see what my future held as I looked in the mirror, but I knew I would somehow make it through this time of uncertainty. You can only truly believe in something if you have faith because reason and physical evidence don't always lead to truth. Think about every time you board a plane, get on a roller-coaster or drive your car. Most of the time you will never see the pilot of the plane or the engineer that constructed the roller-coaster or the car, but you still trust them enough with your life to get in each vehicle with no worries. Everyday, we commit acts of faith without even realizing it.

When I think back on life before becoming a free agent, I realize it was my faith that brought me everything I ever needed. As a child, I was raised in the church, hearing the words of God, which at the time went in one ear and out the other. I would find myself falling asleep no matter how exciting the sermon was, and the worst part was I was usually in front of the entire church when I passed out because I played the drums! Like most children, I was oblivious to the journey that awaited me and how important the words expressed by my pastor, William Harris, would be in my future. I often wondered why people would yell with passion whenever our pastor would say certain things during a sermon. As the years went on, I quickly realized why the words of the Gospel stirred up so many emotions. I began to understand the harsh realities of life, the evil that filled the world, the fact that we are all sinners and the inevitability of death.

I accepted Christianity as my religion through my association with the church, but my faith was not truly built until I was in situations that I could not overcome myself. There will be times when you are left in situations you have no control over and the only option you have is to pray. It is in these moments when we realize how insignificant we are and how great God is. At times, the Lord will completely take you out of your comfort zone and put you in situations where your only choice is to trust in Him. When you eventually overcome these situations, your faith is built because you realize it was only God's grace that helped you make it through.

As I look back, I realize the Lord was preparing me to become a free agent all along and I didn't even know it. It was faith that made me believe my dreams would one day become a reality. That same faith made me understand I could do all things through Christ who strengthened me. He gave me the ability to stay self-motivated and maintain my self-confidence when others would have easily given up. Aside from being someone who was of African descent and a football player, most of all, I was a child of God. That alone gave me my confidence, my identity and self- worth. My faith also helped me develop the fruits of self-control and sacrifice, creating a spirit of gentleness inside of me. In addition, faith allowed me to handle the vigorous trials that came with success and fame, preventing me from becoming prideful and urging me to remain humble. When I would fail, I realized the pain was only temporary and I could overcome any obstacles as long as I kept moving forward and trusting in God. Additionally, giving back became more important as my faith grew. I understood it was better to give than to receive and that whatever was given would be returned. All the lessons I learned over the years had been subconsciously building my faith to the point where it helped me endure the biggest struggle of life; being a free agent. I knew I would be fine whether I played another down of football or not. In my faith, I found peace.

It is my hope that in whatever situation you are going through, that you will put your trust in the Lord's perfect plan. It is always great to have confidence in yourself but there is nothing like the confidence that comes from knowing He will be with you, no matter the highs or lows. In your times of uncertainty as a free agent, you must be able to see past the physical things of this world, keeping your mind focused on the blessings yet to come; realizing there is no shortage of positions on the Lord's team.

EPILOGUE

Rev. Dr. William BGK Harris – Sr. Pastor
(ICF Ministries –Atlanta, GA)

Regardless of who is reading this book, you will agree with me that it is indeed a blessing to your life. In your hands is a valuable tool to motivate and encourage with a few lessons from the life of a young but awesome young man. Certainly Rennie Curran, Jr. is a "diamond in the rough" that has been in the making over the years but is still in the cutting and polishing process of life. No doubt, this humble, dedicated, caring, loving and respected "diamond" has been discovered in many ways and we give thanks to the Creator for his fruitful life. He is very gifted and talented with many unique skills and knowledge including playing the drums, playing great football on the field, serving as a role model for the youths in his Church, neighborhood, campuses, schools, and in others places coupled with his speaking abilities that encourages and motivates people. We anticipate the bright future of this "diamond" that will radiate greater talents and services that will make a difference nationally and international.

On the other hand," life is not a bed of roses" but it comes with various challenges as Rennie discussed herein. Life can be best described as a "roller coaster" that goes up and down or a "swing" that swings forward and backward but often stopping ever now and then. As you have read, Rennie did ride the roller coaster and swing of life but he never gave up when the ride got rocky or when the swing stopped when it was least expected. He demonstrated courage and faith in the midst of every challenge that he faced knowing that "once there is life there is hope". He could have easily became discouraged along the way and turned to things that could destroy his future but he kept faith and hope alive. Moreover, he never forgot where he came from nor did he forget his family and spiritual values. The Creator has kept him for a purpose that will be fulfilled regardless of the obstacles that he will face as stumbling blocks. Nevertheless, it is hard to keep a good man down who is determined to make it against the odds. For sure, the sky is his limit and we pray that all of his dreams will unfold and become alive.

If you are in sports and educational leadership, this book can be a valuable resource. For you who are discouraged, I urge you to take your cues from the lessons of Rennie as you keep pressing forward with faith and confidence. If you are a student in high school or college, particularly if you are into football, you now have a handbook to help you navigate the vast field football and sports. Like Rennie, you too can turn any failures into strength as you strive to overcome your adversities of life. You can't afford to give up for that is not an option at all.

It is important to mention that there have been many hands that picked-up the "diamond" from the rough to encourage, support and motive this young man who has great potentials. I take this opportunity to express my deepest thanks to all of you including his devoted parents and loving family. Rennie, we are all very proud of you and you have not made us ashamed but very proud. Congratulations on your first book and what you have accomplished as we look forward to the next book and the things that you will do as an expression of your dreams!- PEACE!

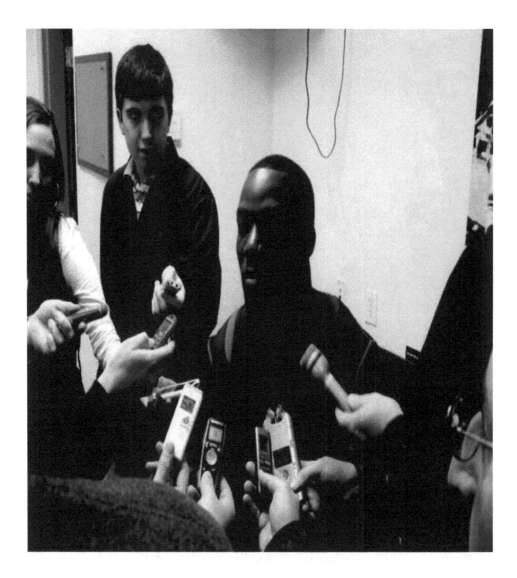

About the Author

Rennie Curran is an internationally acclaimed speaker, author, musician, and multiple award winning former American football linebacker who uses his platform as a professional athlete and entrepreneur empowering audiences to overcome obstacles, stay ahead of the competition, and reach their fullest potential. His experiences of overcoming many circumstances to reach his dream of becoming 3-time All American at The University of Georgia, a 3rd round draft pick with the Tennessee Titans in the NFL Draft, and transitioning into starting his own business gives him a unique perspective on what it takes to handle adversity and maximize opportunities while having a positive impact on others. Through his innovative presentation he teaches organizations how to transform their lives and their business through overcoming adversity, personal branding, and leadership.

Rennie has been counseling and inspiring people for many years. He has been featured on Fox Sports, USA Today, ESPN College Gameday and The Huffington Post.

When Rennie is not training or speaking, he is usually catching up on one his favorite hobbies: music. He grew up playing the piano, drums, and viola. He is also a philanthropist who spends lots of time giving back through several organizations including: Boys and Girls Club, Gifted Foundation, Fellowship of Christian Athletes, MAP Foundation, and many more! He resides in Atlanta, GA.

Curran is both an athletic powerhouse and a determined individual whose prosperity continues to invigorate countless audiences. His drive both on and off the field is a testament to his continuous passion for life. When he's not playing or practicing, Curran spends lots of time with his family, especially his daughter eleana, passing on his wisdom and love to her.

Curran is a man of humility, integrity and resilience.

Contact: Rennie Curran

Former Athlete/Motivational Speaker/Author/Entrepreneur

www.RennieCurran.com | Twitter -@Renniecurran53 | Instagram- @ RennieCurran | Facebook - Facebook.com/RennieCurran53 | Facebook.com/FreeAgentBook | Youtube – Liberandream35

Rennie welcomes opportunities to speak at schools, churches, businesses, conferences, associations, conventions, commencements, retreats, and any other organizational functions